THE KITCHEN

HOME
BAKING

THE KITCHEN LIBRARY
HOME BAKING

Carole Handslip

OCTOPUS BOOKS

CONTENTS

Family Cakes & Sponges	6
Biscuits & Scones	24
Gâteaux	42
Pâtisserie & Small Cakes	52
Breads & Teabreads	66
Festive & Novelty Cakes	82
Index	94

This edition published 1986 by
Octopus Books Limited
59 Grosvenor Street, London W1
Reprinted 1987
© Cathay Books 1980
ISBN 0 7064 2976 1
Printed in Spain

INTRODUCTION

There is nothing quite so appetizing as the warm aroma of freshly baked bread and cakes. Home baking is not the difficult, time-consuming task it is often assumed to be, and the results are most rewarding. With a few well-planned hours in the kitchen, you can produce a delicious variety of tea-time goodies.

For most bread, cake and biscuit making you will need very little equipment. A set of round cake tins, two square ones, a set of sandwich tins and a couple of loaf tins will be sufficient for most of the recipes in this book. For gâteaux, a French *moule a manqué* tin is ideal, as it produces a cake with sloping sides which allows the icing to spread evenly.

Pâtisserie is one area of baking that requires a certain amount of skill; but with practise and attention to detail, it is not difficult to achieve a professional result.

Whether you are experienced at baking or a beginner, the recipes in this book will prove enjoyable to make and the results – delicious!

NOTES

Standard spoon measurements are used in all recipes
1 tablespoon = one 15 ml spoon
1 teaspoon = one 5 ml spoon
All spoon measures are level.

If fresh yeast is unobtainable, substitute dried yeast but use only half the recommended quantity and follow the manufacturer's instructions for reconstituting.

Ovens should be preheated to the specified temperature.

For all recipes, quantities are given in both metric and imperial measures. Follow either set but not a mixture of both, because they are not interchangeable.

FAMILY CAKES & SPONGES

Chocolate Cake

200 g (7 oz) plain flour
1 teaspoon bicarbonate of soda
1 teaspoon baking powder
2 tablespoons cocoa
150 g (5 oz) soft brown sugar
2 tablespoons golden syrup
2 eggs
150 ml (¼ pint) oil
150 ml (¼ pint) milk

CHOCOLATE ICING:
175 g (6 oz) plain chocolate
2 tablespoons single cream

TO DECORATE:
walnut halves
icing sugar

Sift the dry ingredients into a mixing bowl and make a well in the centre. Add the syrup, eggs, oil and milk and beat thoroughly until smooth. Pour into a lined and greased 23 cm (9 inch) cake tin and bake in a preheated moderate oven, 160°C (325°F), Gas Mark 3, for 45 to 50 minutes.

Leave in the tin for a few minutes then turn onto a wire rack to cool.

To make the icing, place the chocolate and cream in a small pan and heat gently until melted. Cool slightly, then pour over the cake. Dredge the walnuts with icing sugar and arrange around the top of the cake.

Makes one 23 cm (9 inch) cake

Ginger Cake

175 g (6 oz) butter or margarine
175 g (6 oz) caster sugar
3 eggs
250 g (8 oz) self-raising flour
½ teaspoon ground ginger
75 g (3 oz) preserved ginger, chopped
2 tablespoons ginger syrup
GINGER ICING:
175 g (6 oz) icing sugar, sifted
2 tablespoons ginger syrup
TO DECORATE:
preserved ginger slices

Cream the fat and sugar together until light and fluffy. Add the eggs one at a time, adding a tablespoon of flour with the last two. Sift and fold in the remaining flour and the ginger, then fold in the preserved ginger and syrup. Turn into a lined and greased 18 cm (7 inch) cake tin.

Bake in a preheated moderate oven, 180°C (350°F), Gas Mark 4, for 1 to 1¼ hours. Turn onto a wire rack to cool.

Beat the icing sugar and syrup together until smooth. Pour over the cake and leave until set. Decorate with ginger slices.

Makes one 18 cm (7 inch) cake

Victoria Sandwich Cake

125 g (4 oz) butter or margarine
125 g (4 oz) caster sugar
2 eggs
125 g (4 oz) self-raising flour, sifted
1 tablespoon hot water
TO FINISH:
3 tablespoons jam
caster sugar

Line and grease two 18 cm (7 inch) sandwich tins.

Cream the fat and sugar together until light and fluffy. Beat in the eggs one at a time, adding a tablespoon of the flour with the second egg. Fold in the remaining flour, then the hot water.

Divide the mixture between the prepared tins and bake in a preheated moderate oven, 180°C (350°F), Gas Mark 4, for 20 to 25 minutes, until the cakes are golden and spring back when lightly pressed. Turn onto a wire rack to cool.

Sandwich the cakes together with the jam and sprinkle the top with caster sugar.

Makes one 18 cm (7 inch) cake

Angel Cake

25 g (1 oz) plain flour
25 g (1 oz) cornflour
150 g (5 oz) caster sugar
5 large egg whites
1 teaspoon vanilla essence
icing sugar for dredging

Sift the flours and 25 g (1 oz) of the caster sugar together 3 or 4 times.

Whisk the egg whites until stiff, add the remaining caster sugar a tablespoon at a time and continue whisking until very thick.

Carefully fold in the sifted mixture with the vanilla essence and turn into a 20 cm (8 inch) angel cake tin. Smooth the surface and bake in a preheated moderate oven, 180°C (350°F), Gas Mark 4, for 35 to 40 minutes, until the cake springs back when lightly pressed.

Turn it upside down on a wire rack and leave in the tin until cold, when the cake will fall easily from the tin. Serve sprinkled with icing sugar.

Makes one 20 cm (8 inch) angel cake

Apple and Cinnamon Cake

300 g (10 oz)
  self-raising flour
1 ½ teaspoons ground
  cinnamon
½ teaspoon salt
250 g (8 oz)
  demerara sugar
50 g (2 oz) raisins
125 g (4 oz) butter,
  melted
2 large eggs, beaten
175 ml (6 fl oz)
  milk
250 g (8 oz) apples,
  peeled, cored and
  chopped
icing sugar for
  dredging

Sift the flour, cinnamon and salt into a bowl and stir in the sugar and raisins. Mix in the melted butter, eggs, milk and apples and beat until smooth.

Turn into a lined and greased 20 cm (8 inch) square cake tin. Bake in a preheated moderate oven, 180°C (350°F), Gas Mark 4, for 1 to 1¼ hours until the cake springs back when lightly pressed.

Turn onto a wire rack to cool, then sprinkle with icing sugar.
Makes one 20 cm (8 inch) cake

Banana Cake

125 g (4 oz) butter or margarine
125 g (4 oz) caster sugar
2 eggs
125 g (4 oz) self-raising flour, sifted
2 bananas, mashed
FILLING:
50 g (2 oz) ground almonds
50 g (2 oz) icing sugar, sifted
1 small banana, mashed
½ teaspoon lemon juice
TO FINISH:
icing sugar

Cream the fat and sugar together until light and fluffy. Add the eggs one at a time, adding a tablespoon of flour with the second egg. Fold in the remaining flour with the bananas.

Divide the mixture between two 18 cm (7 inch) lined and greased sandwich tins. Bake in a preheated moderate oven, 180°C (350°F), Gas Mark 4, for 20 to 25 minutes until the cakes spring back when lightly pressed. Turn onto a wire rack to cool.

To make the filling, mix the ground almonds with the icing sugar, then add the banana and lemon juice and mix to a smooth paste. Sandwich the cakes together with the filling and dredge with icing sugar.

Makes one 18 cm (7 inch) cake

Genoese Sponge

50 g (2 oz) butter
4 eggs
125 g (4 oz) caster sugar
125 g (4 oz) plain flour, sifted
TO FINISH:
150 ml (5 fl oz) double cream
2 tablespoons lemon curd
icing sugar

Warm the butter gently until just soft – do not allow to become oily. Whisk the eggs and sugar in a mixing bowl over a pan of hot water until thick enough to leave a trail. Remove from the heat and whisk until cool. (Hot water is unnecessary if using an electric beater.)

Fold in the flour; when almost incorporated, fold in the butter as rapidly as possible, being careful not to knock out the air. Turn at once into a lined and greased 23 cm (9 inch) moule a manqué tin.

Bake in a preheated moderately hot oven, 190°C (375°F), Gas Mark 5, for 30 to 35 minutes until the cake springs back when lightly pressed. Leave in the tin for 1 minute then turn onto a wire rack to cool.

Whip the cream until stiff then whisk in the lemon curd. Split the cake in half and sandwich together with the lemon cream. Sprinkle with icing sugar.

Makes one 23 cm (9 inch) cake

Whisked Sponge

3 eggs
140 g (4½ oz) caster sugar
75 g (3 oz) plain flour, sifted
TO FINISH:
150 ml (¼ pint) double cream, whipped
2 tablespoons strawberry jam
icing sugar

Line, grease and flour a 23 cm (9 inch) moule a manqué tin.

Whisk the eggs and sugar in a mixing bowl over a pan of boiling water until thick enough to leave a trail. (Hot water is unnecessary if using an electric beater.)

Fold in the flour, then pour into the prepared tin. Bake in a preheated moderately hot oven, 190°C (375°F), Gas Mark 5, for 35 to 40 minutes until the cake springs back when lightly pressed.

Turn onto a wire rack to cool. Split the cake in half, then sandwich together with the cream and jam. Sprinkle with icing sugar.

Makes one 23 cm (9 inch) cake

Swiss Roll

3 eggs
125 g (4 oz) caster sugar
75 g (3 oz) plain flour, sifted
1 tablespoon hot water
3 tablespoons warmed jam
caster sugar for dredging

Line and grease an 18 x 28 cm (7 x 11 inch) Swiss roll tin.

Whisk eggs and sugar in a mixing bowl over a pan of hot water until thick enough to leave a trail. (Hot water is unnecessary if using an electric beater.) Fold in flour and water, then turn into prepared tin.

Bake in a preheated moderately hot oven, 200°C (400°F), Gas Mark 6, for 8 to 10 minutes until the cake springs back when lightly pressed.

Turn onto sugared greaseproof paper, peel off the lining paper and trim the edges. Cut two-thirds of the way through the short edge nearest you, then spread lightly with the jam and roll up quickly. Hold in position for a few minutes, then transfer to a wire rack to cool. Dredge with caster sugar before serving.
Makes one Swiss roll

Cherry Cake

175 g (6 oz) butter or margarine
175 g (6 oz) caster sugar
3 eggs
300 g (10 oz) self-raising flour, sifted
250 g (8 oz) glacé cherries, halved
50 g (2 oz) ground almonds
5 tablespoons milk (approximately)

Line and grease a deep 18 cm (7 inch) cake tin.

Cream the fat and sugar together until light and fluffy. Beat in the eggs one at a time, adding a tablespoon of flour with the last two.

Carefully fold in the remaining flour, then fold in the cherries, almonds and enough milk to give a dropping consistency.

Place in the prepared tin and bake in a preheated moderate oven, 160°C (325°F), Gas Mark 3, for 1½ to 2 hours.

Leave in the tin for 5 minutes, then turn onto a wire rack to cool.

Makes one 18 cm (7 inch) cake

Madeira Cake

250 g (8 oz) plain flour
1 teaspoon baking powder
175 g (6 oz) butter or margarine
175 g (6 oz) caster sugar
grated rind of ½ lemon
3 eggs
2 tablespoons milk
2-3 strips citron peel

Line and grease a deep 18 cm (7 inch) cake tin. Sift the flour and baking powder together and set aside.

Cream the fat and sugar together with the lemon rind until light and fluffy. Beat in the eggs one at a time, adding a tablespoon of flour with the last two. Carefully fold in the remaining flour, then add the milk.

Place the mixture in the prepared tin and bake in a preheated moderate oven, 180°C (350°F), Gas Mark 4, for 1 hour. Arrange the citron peel on top of the cake and bake for a further 30 minutes.

Leave in the tin for 5 minutes, then turn onto a wire rack to cool.
Makes one 18 cm (7 inch) cake

Marmalade Cake

250 g (8 oz) self-raising flour
1 teaspoon ground mixed spice
175 g (6 oz) butter or margarine
175 g (6 oz) soft brown sugar
grated rind and juice of 1 orange
3 eggs
2 tablespoons thick marmalade
75 g (3 oz) mixed dried fruit
2 tablespoons milk
ORANGE ICING:
175 g (6 oz) icing sugar, sifted
grated rind and juice of ½ orange
TO DECORATE:
thinly pared rind of ½ orange, shredded

Line and grease an 18 cm (7 inch) cake tin. Sift the flour and spice together and set aside.

Cream the butter or margarine, sugar and orange rind together until light and fluffy. Beat in the eggs one at a time, adding a tablespoon of flour with the last two. Fold in the marmalade, then fold in the remaining flour with the mixed fruit, orange juice and milk.

Turn into the prepared tin and bake in a preheated moderate oven, 180°C (350°F), Gas Mark 4, for 1¼ to 1½ hours. Leave in the tin for a few minutes, then turn onto a wire rack to cool.

Place the icing ingredients in a bowl and beat until smooth. Pour over the top of the cake; leave until set. Blanch the shredded rind in boiling water, drain thoroughly, then use to decorate the cake.
Makes one 18 cm (7 inch) cake

Dundee Cake

175 g (6 oz) plain flour
1 teaspoon ground mixed spice
125 g (4 oz) butter or margarine
125 g (4 oz) soft brown sugar
grated rind of ½ orange or lemon
3 eggs
125 g (4 oz) sultanas
125 g (4 oz) currants
125 g (4 oz) raisins
50 g (2 oz) glacé cherries, quartered
25 g (1 oz) chopped mixed peel
40 g (1½ oz) split blanched almonds to decorate

Prepare a deep 15 cm (6 inch) cake tin as for Boiled Fruit Cake (see opposite).

Sift the flour and spice together. Cream the fat, sugar and orange rind together until light and fluffy. Beat in the eggs one at a time, adding a tablespoon of flour with the last two. Fold in the remaining flour and the fruit until thoroughly mixed.

Place in the prepared tin, smooth the top and decorate with the almonds. Bake in a preheated moderate oven, 160°C (325°F), Gas Mark 3, for 1 hour, then lower the temperature to 150°C (300°F), Gas Mark 2, and bake for a further 2 to 2½ hours or until a skewer inserted into the centre comes out clean.

Leave in the tin for 5 minutes then turn onto a wire rack to cool.
Makes one 15 cm (6 inch) cake

Farmhouse Fruit Cake

250 g (8 oz) self-raising flour
1 teaspoon ground mixed spice
150 g (5 oz) butter or margarine
150 g (5 oz) soft brown sugar
1 tablespoon black treacle
2 eggs
125 g (4 oz) dates, stoned and chopped
125 g (4 oz) sultanas
125 g (4 oz) currants
25 g (1 oz) chopped mixed peel
3 tablespoons milk

Prepare a deep 18 cm (7 inch) square cake tin as for Boiled Fruit Cake (see opposite). Sift the flour and spice together and set aside.

Cream the butter or margarine, sugar and treacle together until light and fluffy. Beat in the eggs one at a time, adding a tablespoon of flour with the second egg. Fold in the remaining flour with the fruit and milk; mix thoroughly.

Turn into the prepared tin and bake in a preheated moderate oven, 160°C (325°F), Gas Mark 3, for 2 to 2½ hours, or until a skewer inserted into the centre comes out clean.

Leave in the tin for 5 minutes then turn onto a wire rack to cool.
Makes one 18 cm (7 inch) cake

Boiled Fruit Cake

150 g (5 oz) butter or margarine
175 g (6 oz) golden syrup
175 ml (6 fl oz) milk
250 g (8 oz) currants
125 g (4 oz) sultanas
125 g (4 oz) dates, chopped
125 g (4 oz) raisins
50 g (2 oz) chopped mixed peel
250 g (8 oz) plain flour
2 teaspoons ground mixed spice
½ teaspoon bicarbonate of soda
2 eggs, beaten

Grease a deep 18 cm (7 inch) cake tin and line the base and sides with a double layer of greased greaseproof paper. Tie a thick band of brown paper around the outside of the tin and stand it on a pad of brown paper on a baking sheet.

Put the fat, syrup, milk and fruit in a pan and heat slowly until the fat has melted. Simmer gently for 5 minutes, stirring occasionally, then remove from the heat and cool.

Sift the flour, spice and soda into a bowl, add the syrup mixture and the eggs and beat together thoroughly.

Place in the prepared tin and bake in a preheated cool oven, 150°C (300°F), Gas Mark 2, for 2 to 2¼ hours, or until a skewer inserted into the centre comes out clean. Leave in the tin for 5 minutes, then turn onto a wire rack to cool.

Makes one 18 cm (7 inch) cake

Devil's Food Cake

50 g (2 oz) cocoa
200 ml (⅓ pint) boiling water
175 g (6 oz) plain flour
¼ teaspoon baking powder
1 teaspoon bicarbonate of soda
125 g (4 oz) butter or margarine
300 g (10 oz) caster sugar
2 eggs, beaten
BUTTER ICING:
1 tablespoon cocoa
1 tablespoon hot water
50 g (2 oz) butter or margarine
125 g (4 oz) icing sugar, sifted
FUDGE ICING:
50 g (2 oz) butter or margarine
2 tablespoons milk
2 tablespoons cocoa
250 g (8 oz) icing sugar, sifted
TO DECORATE:
8 walnut halves

Line and grease two 20 cm (8 inch) sandwich tins.

Blend the cocoa with half the water until smooth. Stir in the remaining water and leave to cool. Sift the flour, baking powder and soda together.

Cream the fat and sugar and 3 tablespoons of the cocoa mixture together until light and fluffy. Gradually beat in the eggs.

Fold in the flour alternately with the remaining cocoa. The mixture may curdle at this stage but will not affect the result.

Divide the mixture between the prepared cake tins and bake in a preheated moderate oven, 180°C (350°F), Gas Mark 4, for 45 to 50 minutes until firm to the touch. Leave in the tins for 5 minutes, then turn onto a wire rack to cool.

To make the butter icing, blend the cocoa with the hot water, then leave to cool. Beat the butter or margarine with half the icing sugar until light and fluffy. Add the cocoa mixture and remaining icing sugar and beat until smooth. Sandwich the cake layers together with the butter icing.

To make the fudge icing, place the butter or margarine, milk and cocoa in a pan and heat gently until melted. Cool slightly, then add the icing sugar and beat until smooth. Spread over the top and sides of the cake. Decorate with the walnut halves.

Makes one 20 cm (8 inch) cake

Chocolate Almond Cake

125 g (4 oz) plain chocolate
125 g (4 oz) butter or margarine
125 g (4 oz) caster sugar
4 eggs, separated
125 g (4 oz) ground almonds
50 g (2 oz) plain flour, sifted

ICING:
175 g (6 oz) plain chocolate
1 tablespoon water
25 g (1 oz) butter

Melt the chocolate in a basin over a pan of hot water. Cream the fat and sugar together until light and fluffy, then beat in the chocolate. Beat the egg yolks into the creamed mixture, then beat in the almonds and flour.

Whisk the egg whites until stiff and carefully fold into the cake mixture. Pour into a lined and greased 18 cm (7 inch) square cake tin and bake in a preheated moderate oven, 160°C (325°F), Gas Mark 3, for 50 minutes to 1 hour. Leave in the tin for 5 minutes, then cool on a wire rack.

Beat the icing ingredients in a basin over a pan of hot water. Cool slightly, then spread three-quarters of the icing over the cake; leave to set. Place the remaining icing in a small piping bag fitted with a writing nozzle and pipe lines over the top.
Makes one 18 cm (7 inch) cake

Everyday Fruit Cake

250 g (8 oz) self-raising flour
½ teaspoon ground mixed spice
½ teaspoon ground cinnamon
125 g (4 oz) butter or margarine
125 g (4 oz) soft brown sugar
125 g (4 oz) sultanas
125 g (4 oz) currants
50 g (2 oz) glacé cherries, quartered
1 large egg
5 tablespoons milk

Line and grease a deep 15 cm (6 inch) cake tin. Sift the flour and spices into a mixing bowl, add the fat and rub in until the mixture resembles breadcrumbs. Stir in the sugar and fruit. Whisk the egg and milk together, add to the mixture and beat thoroughly.

Place in the prepared tin and bake in a preheated moderate oven, 180°C (350°F), Gas Mark 4, for 1¼ to 1½ hours. Leave in the tin for a few minutes, then turn onto a wire rack to cool.

Makes one 15 cm (6 inch) cake

Crystallized Fruit Cake

175 g (6 oz) butter or margarine
175 g (6 oz) soft brown sugar
250 g (8 oz) plain flour
1 teaspoon ground mixed spice
3 eggs
250 g (8 oz) raisins
125 g (4 oz) sultanas
25 g (1 oz) angelica
125 g (4 oz) glacé cherries, quartered
25 g (1 oz) crystallized ginger
1 tablespoon sherry

TO DECORATE:
75 g (3 oz) crystallized fruits
50 g (2 oz) walnuts

APRICOT GLAZE:
2 tablespoons apricot jam
1 tablespoon water
squeeze of lemon juice

Prepare a deep 18 cm (7 inch) cake tin as for Boiled Fruit Cake (page 17).

Cream the fat and sugar together until light and fluffy. Sift the flour with the mixed spice. Beat in the eggs one at a time, adding a tablespoon of flour with the last two. Fold in the remaining flour with the fruit, ginger and sherry.

Turn into the prepared tin and decorate with the crystallized fruits and walnuts. Bake in a preheated moderate oven, 160°C (325°F), Gas Mark 3, for 1 hour, then lower the temperature to 150°C (300°F), Gas Mark 2, and bake for a further 2 hours until a skewer inserted into the centre comes out clean. Leave in the tin for 5 minutes then turn onto a wire rack to cool.

For the apricot glaze, place the jam and water in a small pan and boil for 3 to 4 minutes. Stir in the lemon juice, then sieve, return to the pan and heat gently. Brush over the fruit.
Makes one 18 cm (7 inch) cake

Sticky Gingerbread

250 g (8 oz) plain flour
3 teaspoons ground ginger
1 teaspoon ground mixed spice
1 teaspoon bicarbonate of soda
125 g (4 oz) butter or margarine
75 g (3 oz) black treacle
125 g (4 oz) golden syrup
50 g (2 oz) soft brown sugar
150 ml (¼ pint) milk
2 eggs, beaten
25 g (1 oz) shredded almonds

Sift the flour, spices and soda into a mixing bowl. Put the fat, treacle, syrup and sugar in a pan and heat gently. Cool slightly then add to the dry ingredients with the milk and eggs and mix thoroughly.

Pour into a lined and greased 18 cm (7 inch) square cake tin, sprinkle with almonds, and bake in a preheated moderate oven, 160°C (325°F), Gas Mark 3, for 1½ to 2 hours or until a skewer inserted into the centre comes out clean.

Leave in the tin for 15 minutes, then turn onto a wire rack to cool. Store in an airtight tin for several days before eating.

Makes one 18 cm (7 inch) cake
NOTE: Replace the ground ginger with finely chopped fresh root ginger, if preferred.

Parkin

250 g (8 oz) wholewheat flour
250 g (8 oz) rolled oats
½ teaspoon bicarbonate of soda
½ teaspoon salt
1 teaspoon ground ginger
125 g (4 oz) butter
125 g (4 oz) black treacle
125 g (4 oz) golden syrup
125 g (4 oz) soft brown sugar
175 ml (6 fl oz) milk

Place the flour and oats in a mixing bowl and sift in the soda, salt and ginger. Place the butter, treacle, syrup and sugar in a saucepan and heat gently. Cool slightly, then add to the dry ingredients, together with the milk; mix thoroughly.

Pour into a lined and greased 20 cm (8 inch) square cake tin and bake in a preheated moderate oven, 180°C (350°F), Gas Mark 4, for 50 to 60 minutes until the cake is firm to the touch.

Leave in the tin for 15 minutes then turn onto a wire rack to cool. Store in an airtight tin for several days before eating.

Makes one 20 cm (8 inch) cake

BISCUITS & SCONES

Macaroons

250 g (8 oz) caster sugar
150 g (5 oz) ground almonds
1 tablespoon rice flour
2 egg whites
rice paper
25 split almonds

Mix the sugar, almonds and rice flour together and set aside. Beat the egg whites lightly, add the dry ingredients, and beat to a smooth, firm consistency.

Leave to stand for 5 minutes then roll into small balls and place slightly apart on a baking sheet lined with rice paper. Flatten slightly and place a split almond on each one.

Bake in a preheated moderate oven, 180°C (350°F), Gas Mark 4, for 20 minutes. Cool on the baking sheet.

Makes 25

Almond Galettes

125 g (4 oz) butter or margarine
50 g (2 oz) caster sugar
1 egg yolk
50 g (2 oz) ground almonds
175 g (6 oz) plain flour

TOPPING:
125 g (4 oz) icing sugar, sifted
1 egg white
50 g (2 oz) shredded almonds

Cream the butter or margarine and sugar together, then add the egg yolk and beat well. Add the ground almonds and flour and mix well. Knead lightly and roll out thinly. Cut into rounds using a 6 cm (2½ inch) plain cutter and place on a greased baking sheet.

For the topping, mix the icing sugar with the egg white, then add the shredded almonds and stir well. Spoon over the biscuits and bake in a preheated moderate oven, 180°C (350°F), Gas Mark 4, for 15 to 20 minutes until golden brown. Cool on the baking sheet.
Makes 24

Oat Crunchies

125 g (4 oz) rolled oats
50 g (2 oz) medium oatmeal
150 g (5 oz) soft brown sugar
120 ml (4 fl oz) vegetable oil
1 egg
½ teaspoon almond essence

Place the oats, oatmeal, sugar and oil in a bowl, mix well and leave to stand for 1 hour. Add the egg and almond essence and beat together thoroughly. Place teaspoonfuls of the mixture well apart on a greased baking sheet and press flat with a damp fork.

Bake in a preheated moderate oven, 160°C (325°F), Gas Mark 3, for 15 to 20 minutes until golden brown. Leave to cool for 2 minutes then transfer to a wire rack to cool completely.
Makes 30

Flapjacks

125 g (4 oz) margarine
125 g (4 oz) soft brown sugar
75 g (3 oz) golden syrup
250 g (8 oz) rolled oats

Melt the margarine with the sugar and syrup, then stir in the rolled oats and mix thoroughly. Turn into a greased shallow 20 cm (8 inch) square tin, and smooth the top with a palette knife.

Bake in a preheated moderate oven, 180°C (350°F), Gas Mark 4, for 25 to 30 minutes until golden brown.

Cool in the tin for 2 minutes, then cut into fingers. Cool completely before removing from the tin.
Makes 16

Chocolate Chip Biscuits

125 g (4 oz) butter or margarine
50 g (2 oz) caster sugar
1 egg, beaten
150 g (5 oz) self-raising flour, sifted
175 g (6 oz) plain chocolate, chopped

Beat the butter or margarine and sugar together until light and fluffy. Add the egg and beat thoroughly. Fold in the flour and chocolate.

Place teaspoonfuls of the mixture a little apart on a greased baking sheet and bake in a preheated moderate oven, 180°C (350°F), Gas Mark 4, for 15 to 20 minutes. Transfer to a wire rack to cool.
Makes 25 to 30

Coconut Cookies

125 g (4 oz) butter
175 g (6 oz) sugar
1 egg, beaten
75 g (3 oz) desiccated coconut
175 g (6 oz) self-raising flour, sifted

Cream the butter until soft, then add the sugar and beat until light and fluffy. Add the egg and beat thoroughly. Add half the coconut and the flour and stir until mixed. Form into small balls and roll in the remaining coconut.

Place slightly apart on a greased baking sheet and flatten with a palette knife. Bake in a preheated moderately hot oven, 190°C (375°F), Gas Mark 5, for 10 to 15 minutes. Transfer to a wire rack to cool.
Makes 40

Cinnamon Crisps

125 g (4 oz) wholewheat flour
50 g (2 oz) rolled oats
75 g (3 oz) sugar
½ teaspoon bicarbonate of soda
1 teaspoon ground cinnamon
75 g (3 oz) butter or margarine
1 tablespoon golden syrup
1 tablespoon milk

Place the flour, oats and sugar in a bowl, sift in the soda and cinnamon and mix thoroughly. Place the butter or margarine, syrup and milk in a pan and heat until the fat has melted. Pour into the dry ingredients and beat until smooth.

Shape into small balls and place slightly apart on a greased baking sheet, flattening with a palette knife.

Bake in a preheated moderate oven, 180°C (350°F), Gas Mark 4, for 15 minutes until golden brown. Cool on the baking sheet.
Makes 25

Date and Oat Slices

175 g (6 oz) wholewheat flour
175 g (6 oz) rolled oats
175 g (6 oz) butter or margarine
50 g (2 oz) soft brown sugar

FILLING:
175 g (6 oz) dates, stoned and chopped
2 tablespoons water
1 tablespoon lemon juice
1 tablespoon clear honey

Place the filling ingredients in a small pan and simmer gently until the dates are soft.

Meanwhile, mix the flour and oats together, then rub in the butter or margarine. Stir in the sugar and place half the mixture in a lined and greased shallow 18 cm (7 inch) square tin, pressing down firmly. Cover with the date mixture, sprinkle over the remaining oat mixture and press down well.

Bake in a preheated moderately hot oven, 190°C (375°F), Gas Mark 5, for 35 to 40 minutes. Cut into slices while warm, then cool completely in the tin before removing carefully.

Makes 12

Digestive Biscuits

175 g (6 oz) wholewheat flour
25 g (1 oz) oatmeal
½ teaspoon salt
1 teaspoon baking powder
75 g (3 oz) butter or margarine
40 g (1½ oz) soft brown sugar
2-3 tablespoons milk

Mix the flour and oatmeal together, then sift in the salt and baking powder. Rub in the butter or margarine until the mixture resembles breadcrumbs, then stir in the sugar. Add the milk and mix to a stiff dough. Roll out thinly, prick well and cut into 6 cm (2½ inch) rounds with a plain cutter.

Place on a greased baking sheet and bake in a preheated moderately hot oven, 190°C (375°F), Gas Mark 5, for 15 to 20 minutes. Transfer to a wire rack to cool. Serve with cheese if liked.
Makes 22

Walnut Cookies

175 g (6 oz) plain flour
1 teaspoon baking powder
½ teaspoon bicarbonate of soda
75 g (3 oz) sugar
75 g (3 oz) butter or margarine
50 g (2 oz) walnuts, chopped
3 tablespoons golden syrup

Sift the flour, baking powder and soda together in a bowl and add the sugar. Rub in the fat until the mixture resembles breadcrumbs, then stir in the walnuts. Add the syrup and mix by hand to a firm dough. Form into balls about the size of a walnut and place slightly apart on a greased baking sheet.

Bake in a preheated moderately hot oven, 190°C (375°F), Gas Mark 5, for 15 minutes until golden brown. Transfer to a wire rack to cool.
Makes 20

Brownies

125 g (4 oz) self-raising flour
¼ teaspoon baking powder
125 g (4 oz) plain chocolate
125 g (4 oz) butter or margarine
125 g (4 oz) soft brown sugar
2 eggs
75 g (3 oz) walnuts, chopped

Sift the flour and baking powder together and set aside. Melt the chocolate in a small bowl over a pan of hot water.

Cream the butter or margarine and sugar together until light and fluffy. Beat in the eggs one at a time, adding a tablespoon of flour with the second egg. Beat in the melted chocolate, then fold in the remaining flour and the walnuts.

Place in a greased and lined shallow 20 cm (8 inch) square tin and bake in a preheated moderate oven, 180°C (350°F), Gas Mark 4, for 30 to 35 minutes.

Cut into squares while still warm, then leave to cool in the tin.
Makes 16

Chocolate Crunch

50 g (2 oz) butter or margarine
50 g (2 oz) golden syrup
125 g (4 oz) plain chocolate
75 g (3 oz) cornflakes
25 g (1 oz) desiccated coconut

Place the butter or margarine, syrup and chocolate in a pan and stir over low heat until melted. Add the cornflakes and coconut and mix well. Turn into a lined and greased 20 cm (8 inch) sandwich tin and chill until set. Cut into wedges to serve.
Makes one 20 cm (8 inch) round

Coconut Pyramids

2 egg whites
150 g (5 oz) caster sugar
150 g (5 oz) desiccated coconut
1 teaspoon cornflour
red food colouring
rice paper

Whisk the egg whites until stiff, then fold in the sugar, coconut and cornflour. Divide the mixture in half and colour one half pink. Place small mounds of the mixture on a baking sheet lined with rice paper and shape into pyramids.

Bake in a preheated moderate oven, 180°C (350°F), Gas Mark 4, for 8 to 10 minutes until lightly browned.
Makes 12

Chocolate Caramel Fingers

125 g (4 oz) butter
50 g (2 oz) caster sugar
175 g (6 oz) plain flour, sifted
CARAMEL FILLING:
125 g (4 oz) butter or margarine
50 g (2 oz) caster sugar
2 tablespoons golden syrup
150 ml (5 fl oz) condensed milk
CHOCOLATE TOPPING:
125 g (4 oz) plain chocolate
15 g (½ oz) butter

Cream the butter and sugar together until light and fluffy. Add the flour and stir until the mixture binds together. Knead until smooth.

Roll out to a square and press evenly into a shallow 20 cm (8 inch) square tin and prick well. Bake in a preheated moderate oven, 180°C (350°F), Gas Mark 4, for 25 to 30 minutes. Cool in the tin.

Place the filling ingredients in a saucepan and stir until dissolved. Bring slowly to the boil, then cook, stirring, for 5 to 7 minutes. Cool slightly, then spread over the biscuit mixture and leave to set.

For the topping, melt the chocolate with the butter over low heat and spread over the caramel. Leave until set, then cut into fingers.

Makes 14

Chocolate Biscuit Cake

125 g (4 oz) margarine
50 g (2 oz) caster sugar
2 tablespoons golden syrup
2 tablespoons milk
2 tablespoons drinking chocolate
1 tablespoon cocoa
250 g (8 oz) digestive biscuits, crushed
50 g (2 oz) cake crumbs
50 g (2 oz) glacé cherries, chopped
50 g (2 oz) raisins
CHOCOLATE ICING:
125 g (4 oz) plain chocolate
15 g (½ oz) butter

Place the margarine, sugar, syrup and milk in a pan and heat gently. Add the drinking chocolate, cocoa and half the biscuits and mix well. Add the remaining ingredients and stir until thoroughly mixed, then press into a 20 cm (8 inch) sandwich tin. Chill in the refrigerator until set, then remove from the tin.

Melt the chocolate and butter in a small bowl over a pan of hot water and mix well. Spread over the biscuit mixture and allow to set, then cut into wedges.

Makes one 20 cm (8 inch) round

Ginger Nuts

50 g (2 oz) butter or margarine
4 tablespoons golden syrup
50 g (2 oz) soft brown sugar
175 g (6 oz) self-raising flour
1 teaspoon ground ginger

Melt the butter or margarine, syrup and sugar together in a saucepan. Cool, then sift in the flour and ginger and mix to a smooth paste. Roll into small balls the size of a walnut, place well apart on a greased baking sheet and flatten slightly.

Bake in a preheated moderately hot oven, 190°C (375°F), Gas Mark 5, for 15 to 20 minutes. Leave on the sheet for 1 minute, then transfer to a wire rack to cool.
Makes 25 to 30

Uncooked Chocolate Bars

50 g (2 oz) butter or margarine
200 g (7 oz) plain chocolate
3 tablespoons golden syrup
250 g (8 oz) digestive biscuits, crushed

Place the butter or margarine, chocolate and syrup in a saucepan and heat gently until melted. Stir in the biscuits and mix thoroughly.

Turn into a greased and lined shallow 18 cm (7 inch) square tin and smooth the top with a palette knife. Leave to set, then cut into bars.
Makes 16

Chocolate Crisps

125 g (4 oz) butter or margarine
50 g (2 oz) caster sugar
125 g (4 oz) self-raising flour
25 g (1 oz) cocoa

Beat the butter or margarine and sugar together until light and fluffy. Sift in the flour and cocoa and mix well. Form into small balls about the size of a walnut, place on a greased baking sheet and flatten with a damp fork. Bake in a preheated moderately hot oven, 190°C (375°F), Gas Mark 5, for 10 to 15 minutes. Transfer to a wire rack to cool.
Makes 24

Wholewheat Biscuits

75 g (3 oz) self-raising flour
½ teaspoon ground mixed spice
75 g (3 oz) wholewheat flour
25 g (1 oz) oatmeal
125 g (4 oz) butter or margarine
50 g (2 oz) demerara sugar
2 tablespoons milk

Sift the flour and spice into a bowl, then stir in the wholewheat flour and oatmeal. Rub in the fat until the mixture resembles breadcrumbs, add the sugar and mix to a firm dough with the milk.

Turn onto a floured surface, knead lightly then roll out very thinly. Cut into 7.5 cm (3 inch) rounds using a fluted cutter and place on a greased baking sheet. Bake in a preheated moderately hot oven, 190°C (375°F), Gas Mark 5, for 15 minutes. Transfer to a wire rack to cool.
Makes 18 to 20

Scones

250 g (8 oz) plain flour
1 teaspoon cream of tartar
½ teaspoon bicarbonate of soda
½ teaspoon salt
50 g (2 oz) butter or margarine
25 g (1 oz) caster sugar
120 ml (4 fl oz) milk
milk to glaze

Sift the flour, cream of tartar, soda and salt into a mixing bowl and rub in the butter or margarine until the mixture resembles breadcrumbs. Stir in the sugar, add the milk and mix to a soft dough.

Turn onto a floured surface, knead lightly and roll out to a 2 cm (¾ inch) thickness. Cut into 5 cm (2 inch) rounds with a fluted cutter. Place on a floured baking sheet and brush with milk. Bake in a preheated hot oven, 220°C (425°F), Gas Mark 7, for 12 to 15 minutes. Transfer to a wire rack to cool. Serve with jam and butter or cream.

Makes 12 to 14

DATE SCONES: Sift ½ teaspoon ground cinnamon with the flour and mix in 50 g (2 oz) finely chopped dates with the sugar.

WHOLEWHEAT SCONES: Replace 125 g (4 oz) plain flour with 125 g (4 oz) wholewheat flour.

Fruit Scone Round

250 g (8 oz) self-raising flour
1 teaspoon baking powder
50 g (2 oz) butter or margarine
25 g (1 oz) caster sugar
75 g (3 oz) currants or sultanas
120 ml (4 fl oz) milk
milk to glaze

Sift the flour and baking powder into a bowl and rub in the fat until the mixture resembles breadcrumbs. Stir in the sugar and fruit, add the milk and mix to a soft dough.

Turn onto a floured surface, knead lightly then form into an 18 cm (7 inch) round and place on a floured baking sheet.

Score the round into 8 sections, brush with milk and bake in a preheated moderately hot oven, 200°C (400°F), Gas Mark 6, for 15 to 20 minutes until golden brown. Transfer to a wire rack to cool and serve with butter and jam.

Makes one 18 cm (7 inch) round

Cheese-Topped Scones

250 g (8 oz) self-raising flour
1 teaspoon mustard
pinch of cayenne pepper
½ teaspoon salt
50 g (2 oz) butter or margarine
125 g (4 oz) cheese, grated
1 egg, beaten
4 tablespoons milk
milk to glaze

Sift the flour, mustard, cayenne and salt into a bowl and rub in the fat until the mixture resembles breadcrumbs. Stir in 75 g (3 oz) of the cheese, the egg and milk and mix to a soft dough.

Turn onto a floured surface, knead lightly and roll out to a 2 cm (¾ inch) thickness. Cut into 5 cm (2 inch) rounds with a plain cutter and place on a floured baking sheet. Brush with milk and sprinkle with the remaining cheese.

Bake in a preheated moderately hot oven, 200°C (400°F), Gas Mark 6, for 15 to 20 minutes. Transfer to a wire rack to cool. Serve with butter.
Makes 10

Drop Scones

250 g (8 oz) plain flour
1 teaspoon cream of tartar
½ teaspoon bicarbonate of soda
½ teaspoon salt
25 g (1 oz) caster sugar
1 large egg
250 ml (8 fl oz) milk
1 tablespoon oil

Sift the dry ingredients together into a mixing bowl and make a well in the centre. Add the egg and half the milk and mix to a smooth batter. Gradually beat in the remaining milk with the oil, mixing to a thick batter.

Heat a heavy frying pan or griddle and grease lightly. Drop tablespoonfuls of the batter onto the griddle and cook until the top is blistered. Turn with a palette knife and cook until the underside is golden brown. Place the scones inside a clean folded tea-towel to keep moist until they are all cooked. Serve with butter.

Makes 12 to 16

Shortbread

125 g (4 oz) butter
50 g (2 oz) caster sugar
175 g (6 oz) plain flour, sifted
caster sugar for dredging

Cream the butter and sugar together until light and fluffy. Add the flour and stir until the mixture binds together.

Turn onto a lightly floured board and knead until smooth. Roll out to a 20 cm (8 inch) round and place on a greased baking sheet. Pinch the edges with your fingers, prick well with a fork and mark into 8 portions.

Dust with caster sugar and bake in a preheated moderate oven, 160°C (325°F), Gas Mark 3, for 40 to 45 minutes until pale golden. Leave on the baking sheet for 5 minutes, then transfer to a wire rack to cool completely.
Makes one 20 cm (8 inch) round

GÂTEAUX

Chocolate and Chestnut Gâteau

75 g (3 oz) plain chocolate
2 tablespoons water
4 eggs, separated
250 g (8 oz) caster sugar
350 g (12 oz) chestnuts, cooked and sieved

TO FINISH:
284 ml (10 fl oz) double cream, whipped
1 marron glacé

Melt the chocolate and water in a bowl over a pan of hot water. Add the egg yolks and sugar and whisk until thick enough to leave a trail. Whisk the egg whites until stiff, then fold into the mixture with the chestnuts.

Turn into two lined and greased 20 cm (8 inch) sandwich tins and bake in a preheated moderate oven, 180°C (350°F), Gas Mark 4, for 35 to 40 minutes. Leave for a few minutes, then turn onto a wire rack to cool.

Use half the cream to sandwich the cakes together. Spread 2 tablespoons cream over the top of the cake and pipe the remainder in rosettes to decorate. Place a piece of marron glacé on each rosette.

Makes one 20 cm (8 inch) gâteau

Gâteau Normande

WHISKED SPONGE:
3 eggs
140 g (4½ oz) caster sugar
75 g (3 oz) plain flour, sifted
1 teaspoon ground mixed spice

FILLING AND TOPPING:
500 g (1 lb) apples, peeled, cored and sliced
2 tablespoons apricot jam
50 g (2 oz) sultanas
50 g (2 oz) raisins
2 tablespoons soft brown sugar
284 ml (10 fl oz) double cream, whipped

Prepare and bake the sponge as for Whisked Sponge (page 12), adding the spice with the flour.

Place the apples and apricot jam in a pan, cover and cook over a gentle heat until soft. Stir in the dried fruit and sugar, then leave to cool.

Split the cake in half and sandwich together with the apple filling and one third of the cream.

Swirl another third of the cream over the top of the cake and pipe the remainder in rosettes around the edge.

Makes one 23 cm (9 inch) gâteau

Gâteau au Chocolat

3 eggs
140 g (4½ oz) caster sugar
50 g (2 oz) plain flour
25 g (1 oz) cocoa
CHOCOLATE CARAQUE:
75 g (3 oz) plain chocolate
BUTTER CREAM:
2 egg whites
125 g (4 oz) icing sugar
125 g (4 oz) unsalted butter
50 g (2 oz) plain chocolate, melted

Line and grease a 23 cm (9 inch) moule a manqué tin.

Place the eggs and sugar in a bowl and whisk over a pan of boiling water until thickened. (The hot water is unnecessary if using an electric beater.) Sift and fold in the flour and cocoa. Pour into the prepared tin and bake in a preheated moderately hot oven, 190°C (375°F), Gas Mark 5, for 35 to 40 minutes. Turn onto a wire rack to cool.

To make the caraque, melt the chocolate on a plate over a pan of hot water. Spread thinly on a board and leave until nearly set, then shave it off into curls with a sharp knife.

Make the butter cream as for Gâteau Moka (page 47), flavouring with the melted chocolate instead of coffee essence.

Split the cake in half, sandwich together with some of the butter cream and use the rest to cover the cake. Decorate with the chocolate.
Makes one 23 cm (9 inch) gâteau

Gâteau Pithiviers

75 g (3 oz) ground almonds
75 g (3 oz) caster sugar
40 g (1½ oz) butter or margarine
1 egg
25 g (1 oz) plain flour, sifted
½ teaspoon almond essence
368 g (13 oz) packet frozen puff pastry, thawed
TO GLAZE:
1 egg white
1 tablespoon caster sugar

Mix the almonds with the sugar, fat and egg and beat well. Stir in the flour and almond essence.

Roll out the pastry and cut into two 20 cm (8 inch) rounds, one slightly thicker than the other. Place the thin round on a dampened baking sheet and cover with the almond filling, leaving a 2.5 cm (1 inch) border. Dampen the edge of the pastry and place the thicker round on top. Press the edges together and knock up with the back of a knife.

Decorate with curved cuts in the shape of a wheel. Brush with egg white and sprinkle with the caster sugar. Bake in a preheated hot oven, 220°C (425°F), Gas Mark 7, for 25 to 30 minutes. Transfer to a wire rack to cool.

Makes one 20 cm (8 inch) gâteau

Gâteau aux Fraises

3 eggs, separated
125 g (4 oz) caster sugar
grated rind and juice of ½ lemon
50 g (2 oz) semolina
25 g (1 oz) ground almonds
TO FINISH:
284 ml (10 fl oz) double cream, whipped
250 g (8 oz) strawberries, halved
4 tablespoons redcurrant jelly
2 teaspoons water
50 g (2 oz) almonds, chopped and browned

Cream the egg yolks with the sugar, lemon rind and juice until thick. Stir in the semolina and ground almonds, then fold in the stiffly whisked egg whites. Turn the mixture into a lined, greased and floured 23 cm (9 inch) moule a manqué tin and bake in a preheated moderate oven, 180°C (350°F), Gas Mark 4, for 35 to 40 minutes. Turn onto a wire rack to cool.

Split the cake in half and sandwich together with three-quarters of the cream. Arrange the strawberries on the top.

Heat the redcurrant jelly with the water, sieve, reheat and use to glaze the strawberries and side of the cake. Press the browned almonds around the side and pipe the remaining cream around the top to decorate.

Makes one 23 cm (9 inch) gâteau

Gâteau Moka

GENOESE SPONGE:
50 g (2 oz) butter
4 eggs
125 g (4 oz) caster sugar
125 g (4 oz) plain flour, sifted

BUTTER CREAM:
2 egg whites
125 g (4 oz) icing sugar, sifted
125 g (4 oz) unsalted butter
1 tablespoon coffee essence

TO DECORATE:
125 g (4 oz) flaked almonds
icing sugar

Prepare and bake the sponge as for Genoese Sponge (page 12).

To make the butter cream, whisk the egg whites and icing sugar together over a pan of simmering water until the mixture holds its shape. Cool slightly. Cream the butter until soft, then add the meringue mixture a little at a time. Flavour with the coffee essence.

Split the sponge in half and sandwich together with some of the butter cream.

Spread the remaining butter cream all over the cake and decorate with the almonds. Sift a little icing sugar over the top.

Makes one 23 cm (9 inch) gâteau

Caramel Chip Gâteau

125 g (4 oz) butter or margarine
175 g (6 oz) soft brown sugar
3 eggs
250 g (8 oz) self-raising flour, sifted
4 tablespoons hot black coffee
CARAMEL CHIPS:
175 g (6 oz) caster sugar
FILLING:
50 g (2 oz) butter
125 g (4 oz) icing sugar, sifted
2 tablespoons milk
ICING:
350 g (12 oz) icing sugar, sifted
1 tablespoon coffee essence
2 tablespoons water

Cream the fat until soft then add the sugar and beat thoroughly. Add the eggs one at a time, adding a tablespoon of flour with each one.

Fold in the remaining flour with the coffee, then turn into two lined and greased 20 cm (8 inch) sandwich tins. Bake in a preheated moderate oven, 180°C (350°F), Gas Mark 4, for 25 to 30 minutes. Turn onto a wire rack to cool.

To make the caramel chips, place the sugar in a small pan and heat gently until dissolved. Boil until it forms a golden brown caramel and pour immediately onto a greased baking sheet. When cool, break the caramel into small pieces. Set aside about half for decorating. Crush the remainder finely with a rolling pin.

To make the filling, cream the butter and icing sugar together, add a tablespoon of finely crushed caramel and mix to a soft consistency with the milk. Use to sandwich the cakes together.

To make the icing, mix the icing sugar with the coffee essence and water. Pour over the cake and decorate with the remaining caramel chips.

Makes one 20 cm (8 inch) gâteau

Gâteau aux Noisettes

125 g (4 oz) caster sugar
3 eggs
50 g (2 oz) plain flour, sifted
50 g (2 oz) ground hazelnuts, browned
1 tablespoon oil
BUTTER CREAM:
2 egg whites
125 g (4 oz) icing sugar
125 g (4 oz) unsalted butter
1 tablespoon coffee essence
PRALINE POWDER:
50 g (2 oz) unblanched almonds
50 g (2 oz) caster sugar
ICING:
175 g (6 oz) icing sugar, sifted
2 teaspoons coffee essence
2 teaspoons water

Whisk the sugar and eggs together in a bowl until thick enough to leave a trail. Fold in the flour, hazelnuts and oil.

Turn into a lined and greased 23 cm (9 inch) moule a manqué tin and bake in a preheated moderately hot oven, 190°C (375°F), Gas Mark 5, for 25 to 30 minutes until the cake springs back when lightly pressed. Turn onto a wire rack to cool, then split in half.

Make the butter cream as for Gâteau Moka (page 47) and the praline powder as for Apricot Gâteau (page 51).

Mix 2 tablespoons praline into the butter cream. Use 3 tablespoons of this to sandwich the sponge together. Spread more butter cream around the side of the cake and press the remaining praline onto it.

For the icing, mix the icing sugar with the coffee essence and water until smooth. Spread over the top of the cake and leave to set.

Pipe the remaining butter cream in a border around the top edge.

Makes one 23 cm (9 inch) gâteau

Coffee and Walnut Layer Cake

4 eggs
175 g (6 oz) caster sugar
125 g (4 oz) plain flour, sifted
1 tablespoon oil
125 g (4 oz) walnuts, finely chopped
BUTTER ICING:
250 g (8 oz) butter
500 g (1 lb) icing sugar, sifted
2 tablespoons milk
2 tablespoons coffee essence
TO DECORATE:
walnut halves

Line and grease two 20 cm (8 inch) sandwich tins. Whisk the eggs and sugar in a bowl over a pan of boiling water until thick enough to leave a trail. (If using an electric beater, the hot water is unnecessary.)

Partially fold in the flour, then add the oil and chopped walnuts and fold in gently. Divide between the prepared tins and bake in a preheated moderately hot oven, 190°C (375°F), Gas Mark 5, for 30 to 35 minutes until the cakes spring back when lightly pressed. Turn onto a wire rack to cool. Split each cake in half.

To make the butter icing, cream the fat with half the icing sugar until soft, then add the milk, essence and remaining icing sugar. Beat well.

Spread a quarter of the icing onto three of the cake rounds and sandwich the cake together. Swirl the remaining icing over the cake and decorate with walnut halves.
Makes one 20 cm (8 inch) cake

Apricot Gâteau

SPONGE:
3 eggs
125 g (4 oz) caster sugar
grated rind and juice of 1 lemon
50 g (2 oz) semolina
25 g (1 oz) ground almonds

PRALINE POWDER:
50 g (2 oz) almonds (unblanched)
50 g (2 oz) caster sugar

TO FINISH:
170 ml (6 fl oz) double cream
411 g (14½ oz) can apricot halves
4 tablespoons apricot glaze (see page 54)

Make the sponge as for Gâteau aux Fraises (page 46).

Place the unblanched almonds and sugar in a pan and heat very gently until the sugar melts. Stir with a metal spoon and cook until it is a nut brown colour. Turn onto an oiled baking sheet to cool, then crush to a coarse powder.

Whip the cream and fold in 2 tablespoons of the praline powder. Split the sponge in half and sandwich together with the praline cream. Arrange the apricots on top. Brush the glaze over the apricots and side of the gâteau and press the remaining praline round the side.

Makes one 23 cm (9 inch) gâteau

PÂTISSERIE & SMALL CAKES

Walnut Meringues

2 egg whites
125 g (4 oz) icing sugar, sifted
50 g (2 oz) walnuts, finely chopped

Whisk the egg whites until stiff and dry. Add the icing sugar a tablespoon at a time and continue to whisk until very thick.

Carefully fold in the walnuts. Place small mounds of the mixture on a baking sheet lined with non-stick paper.

Bake in a preheated moderate oven, 180°C (350°F), Gas Mark 4, for 15 to 20 minutes. Leave to cool slightly, then carefully transfer to a wire rack to cool completely.
Makes 22

Florentines

75 g (3 oz) butter
75 g (3 oz) golden syrup
25 g (1 oz) plain flour
75 g (3 oz) flaked almonds, coarsely chopped
25 g (1 oz) chopped mixed peel
50 g (2 oz) glacé cherries, coarsely chopped
1 teaspoon lemon juice
125 g (4 oz) plain chocolate

Melt the butter and syrup in a small pan, then stir in the flour, almonds, mixed peel, cherries and lemon juice.
Place teaspoonfuls of the mixture well apart on baking sheets lined with non-stick paper. Flatten with a fork and bake in a preheated moderate oven, 180°C (350°F), Gas Mark 4, for 8 to 10 minutes. Transfer to a wire rack to cool.
Melt the chocolate in a bowl over a pan of hot water, then spread over the flat underside of each florentine. Place the biscuits chocolate side up on a wire rack and mark the chocolate into wavy lines with a fork. Leave until set.
Makes 14

Mocha Slices

GENOESE SPONGE:
25 g (1 oz) butter
2 eggs
50 g (2 oz) caster sugar
50 g (2 oz) plain flour, sifted
BUTTER CREAM:
2 egg whites
125 g (4 oz) icing sugar, sifted
125 g (4 oz) unsalted butter
1 tablespoon coffee essence
APRICOT GLAZE:
4 tablespoons apricot jam
3 tablespoons water
squeeze of lemon juice
ICING:
250 g (8 oz) icing sugar, sifted
2 teaspoons coffee essence
1 ½ tablespoons water

Prepare the sponge as for Genoese Sponge (page 12). Turn into a lined and greased 18 cm (7 inch) square shallow tin and bake in a preheated moderately hot oven, 190°C (375°F), Gas Mark 5, for 25 to 30 minutes. Turn onto a wire rack to cool, then split in half.

Prepare the butter cream as for Gâteau Moka (page 47), and use some to sandwich the cake together. Cut the cake into fingers, 7.5 x 2.5 cm (3 x 1 inch).

To make the apricot glaze, heat the jam and water in a small pan and boil for 3 to 4 minutes. Add the lemon juice, sieve, then reheat and brush over the fingers to coat completely. Leave to set.

To make the icing, combine the icing sugar, coffee essence and water, then spread over the fingers and leave to set.

Pipe the remaining butter cream along the middle of each slice.
Makes 10

Langues de Chats

50 g (2 oz) butter
50 g (2 oz) caster sugar
2 egg whites
50 g (2 oz) plain flour, sifted
vanilla essence

Cream the butter and sugar together until light and fluffy. Whisk the egg whites lightly and gradually beat into the creamed mixture. Carefully fold in the flour and essence.

Place in a piping bag fitted with a 1 cm (⅜ inch) plain nozzle and pipe 7.5 cm (3 inch) lengths on a greased and floured baking sheet. Bake in a preheated moderately hot oven, 200°C (400°F), Gas Mark 6, for 10 minutes; the biscuits should be pale golden but darker around the edges. Transfer to a wire rack to cool.
Makes 20 to 24

Viennese Fingers

175 g (6 oz) butter or margarine
50 g (2 oz) icing sugar
grated rind of 1 orange
125 g (4 oz) plain flour
50 g (2 oz) cornflour
2 tablespoons apricot jam
75 g (3 oz) plain chocolate

Cream the butter or margarine and sugar together with the orange rind until light and fluffy.

Sift in the flour and cornflour and beat well. Place in a piping bag fitted with a 2.5 cm (1 inch) fluted nozzle, and pipe 7.5 cm (3 inch) fingers well apart on a baking sheet lined with non-stick paper.

Bake in a preheated moderate oven, 180°C (350°F), Gas Mark 4, for 15 minutes. Transfer to a wire rack to cool. Sandwich the fingers together in pairs with a little jam.

Melt the chocolate in a small bowl over a pan of hot water. Dip both ends of the fingers in the chocolate and place on a piece of greaseproof paper. Leave until set.
Makes 12

Japonais

50 g (2 oz) ground almonds
125 g (4 oz) caster sugar
2 egg whites
BUTTER ICING:
75 g (3 oz) butter
175 g (6 oz) icing sugar, sifted
1 teaspoon coffee essence
1 tablespoon milk
GLACÉ ICING:
125 g (4 oz) icing sugar, sifted
1 teaspoon coffee essence
2 teaspoons water
TO FINISH:
25 g (1 oz) ground almonds, browned
8 hazelnuts, toasted and skinned

Mix the almonds and sugar together and set aside. Whisk the egg whites until stiff, then fold in the almonds and sugar. Spoon the mixture into a piping bag fitted with a 1 cm (½ inch) plain nozzle and pipe 16 5 cm (2 inch) rounds on non-stick paper placed on a baking sheet. Bake in a preheated cool oven, 150°C (300°F), Gas Mark 2, for 30 to 35 minutes. Transfer to a wire rack to cool.

Make the butter icing as for Coffee Walnut Layer Cake (page 50). Sandwich the rounds together in pairs with some of the icing and spread more round the sides.

To make the glacé icing, mix the icing sugar with the coffee essence and water until smooth.

Press ground almonds round the side of each cake. Place a teaspoon of the glacé icing on top and spread to the edge. Leave to set, then decorate with piped rosettes of the remaining butter icing and hazelnuts.
Makes 8

Chocolate Éclairs

50 g (2 oz) butter or margarine
150 ml (¼ pint) water
65 g (2½ oz) plain flour, sifted
2 eggs, beaten
170 ml (6 fl oz) double cream, whipped

ICING:
125 g (4 oz) plain chocolate
15 g (½ oz) butter

Melt the butter or margarine in a saucepan over a gentle heat. Add the water and bring to the boil. Remove from the heat, add the flour all at once and beat well until the mixture leaves the sides of the pan clean. Cool slightly, then add the eggs a little at a time, beating well between each addition.

Spoon the mixture into a piping bag fitted with a 1 cm (½ inch) plain nozzle and pipe 7.5 cm (3 inch) lengths onto a dampened baking sheet. Bake in a preheated moderately hot oven, 200°C (400°F), Gas Mark 6, for 25 minutes until crisp and golden brown. Make a slit in the side of each éclair to allow the steam to escape and cool on a wire rack.

Fill a piping bag fitted with a 1 cm (½ inch) plain nozzle with the cream and pipe a little into each éclair.

Melt the chocolate and butter on a plate over a pan of hot water and mix well. Dip each éclair into the chocolate; place on a wire rack to set.
Makes 10 to 12

Tartelettes aux Fraises

PÂTE SUCRÉE:
125 g (4 oz) plain flour
50 g (2 oz) butter, softened
50 g (2 oz) caster sugar
2 egg yolks
few drops of vanilla essence
GLAZE:
4 tablespoons redcurrant jelly
1 tablespoon water
FILLING:
250 g (8 oz) strawberries

Sift the flour onto a board, make a well in the centre and place the butter, sugar, egg yolks and vanilla in the well. Using the fingertips of one hand, work these ingredients together until well blended, then draw in the flour. Knead lightly until smooth and chill for 1 hour.

Roll out the pastry very thinly and use to line 14 patty tins, then press a square of foil into each. Bake blind in a preheated moderately hot oven, 190°C (375°F), Gas Mark 5, for 10 minutes or until golden. Cool, then remove foil and turn out.

To make the glaze, heat the redcurrant jelly with the water. Bring to the boil, then sieve and reheat. Brush the cases with glaze. Arrange the fruit in the cases and brush with the remaining glaze.
Makes 14

Cream Horns

212 g (7½ oz) packet frozen puff pastry, thawed
beaten egg to glaze
strawberry jam
170 ml (6 fl oz) double cream, whipped
TO DECORATE:
cherries and angelica
icing sugar

Roll out the pastry into a rectangle about 25 x 33 cm (10 x 13 inches) and trim the edges. Cut into 10 strips 2.5 cm (1 inch) wide. Dampen one long edge of each strip with water and wind round 10 cornet moulds, starting at the point and overlapping the dampened edge. Gently press the edges together. Place on a dampened baking sheet and chill for 15 minutes.

Brush with egg and bake in a preheated hot oven, 220°C (425°F), Gas Mark 7, for 15 to 20 minutes until golden brown. Leave for 5 minutes before carefully removing the moulds. Cool on a wire rack.

Spoon a little jam into each horn then pipe in the cream. Decorate with a piece of cherry and angelica and sprinkle with icing sugar.
Makes 10

Walnut Barquettes

PÂTE SUCRÉE:
125 g (4 oz) plain flour
50g (2 oz) butter, softened
50 g (2 oz) caster sugar
2 egg yolks
few drops vanilla essence

WALNUT FILLING:
50 g (2 oz) butter
50 g (2 oz) caster sugar
1 egg, beaten
25 g (1 oz) plain flour, sifted
50 g (2 oz) walnuts, ground

ICING:
125 g (4 oz) icing sugar, sifted
1 egg white

Make the pâte sucrée as for Tartelettes aux Fraises (opposite). Roll out thinly and use to line 14 barquette moulds. Prick and chill for 20 minutes.

To make the walnut filling, cream the butter and sugar together until light and fluffy, then add the egg and flour and beat well. Fold in the walnuts, spoon the mixture into a piping bag fitted with a plain nozzle and pipe into the pastry cases.

To make the icing, mix the icing sugar with the egg white until smooth. Spoon into a piping bag fitted with a writing nozzle and pipe a criss-cross pattern over each cake.

Bake in a preheated moderately hot oven, 200°C (400°F), Gas Mark 6, for 20 minutes. Leave in the moulds for 5 minutes, then transfer to a wire rack to cool.
Makes 14

Brandy Snaps

125 g (4 oz) butter
125 g (4 oz) demerara sugar
125 g (4 oz) golden syrup
125 g (4 oz) plain flour
1 teaspoon ground ginger

Put the butter, sugar and syrup into a saucepan and heat gently until the butter has melted and the sugar dissolved. Cool slightly, then sift in the flour and ginger and beat well.

Place teaspoonfuls of the mixture on a greased baking sheet at least 10 cm (4 inches) apart. Bake in a preheated moderate oven, 180°C (350°F), Gas Mark 4, for 10 to 12 minutes until golden.

Leave to cool slightly then remove with a palette knife and roll round the greased handle of a wooden spoon. Leave for 1 to 2 minutes to set, then slip them off carefully onto a wire rack to cool. Serve plain or filled with whipped cream.

Makes 35

NOTE: If the biscuits cool too much and are too brittle to roll, return to the oven for 1 minute to soften.

Frangipane Tartlets

SHORTCRUST PASTRY:
25g (1 oz) butter
25g (1 oz) lard
125g (4 oz) plain flour, sifted
water to mix

FILLING:
50 g (2 oz) butter
50 g (2 oz) caster sugar
1 egg, beaten
1 tablespoon flour
50 g (2 oz) ground almonds
2 drops of almond essence
25 g (1 oz) flaked almonds
2 tablespoons apricot glaze (see page 21)

To make the pastry, rub the fat into the flour until the mixture resembles breadcrumbs. Stir in enough water to make a firm dough. Knead lightly, cover and chill for 30 minutes.

Roll out thinly, cut into ten 7.5 cm (3 inch) circles and use to line 10 deep patty tins. Chill for 15 minutes.

Cream the butter and sugar together until light and fluffy, add the egg, then beat in the flour. Mix in the almonds and essence, then spoon into a piping bag fitted with a 1 cm (½ inch) plain nozzle and two-thirds fill the pastry cases. Sprinkle with flaked almonds and bake in a preheated moderately hot oven, 200°C (400°F), Gas Mark 6, for 20 minutes. Transfer to a wire rack then brush with the glaze.

Makes 10

Sponge Fingers

50 g (2 oz) caster sugar
2 eggs
vanilla essence
50 g (2 oz) plain flour, sifted
caster sugar for dredging

Whisk the sugar, eggs and vanilla essence in a mixing bowl over a pan of hot water until thick. (If using an electric beater, the hot water is unnecessary.) Fold in the flour.

Place the mixture in a piping bag fitted with a 1 cm (½ inch) plain nozzle and pipe into finger lengths on greased and floured baking sheets. Dust well with caster sugar and bake in a preheated moderately hot oven, 190°C (375°F), Gas Mark 5, for 6 to 8 minutes until golden brown. Transfer to a wire rack to cool.
Makes 22

Almond Curls

75 g (3 oz) butter
75 g (3 oz) caster sugar
50 g (2 oz) plain flour, sifted
75 g (3 oz) flaked almonds

Cream the butter and sugar together until light and fluffy. Stir in the flour and almonds and mix well. Place teaspoonfuls of the mixture well apart on a greased baking sheet and flatten with a damp fork.

Bake in a preheated moderately hot oven, 200°C (400°F), Gas Mark 6, for 6 to 8 minutes until pale golden. Leave on the baking sheet for 1 minute, then remove with a palette knife and place on a rolling pin to curl. Leave until set in a curl, then remove very carefully.
Makes 25

Tea-Time Truffles

300 g (10 oz) cake crumbs
50 g (2 oz) caster sugar
2 tablespoons cocoa
3 tablespoons apricot jam
1 tablespoon rum
4 tablespoons chocolate vermicelli

Mix the cake crumbs, sugar and cocoa together in a bowl. Add the jam and rum and mix to a stiff paste. Form into balls the size of a walnut and roll in the chocolate vermicelli. Serve in paper cases.
Makes 15

Strawberry Palmiers

212 g (7½ oz)
  packet frozen puff
  pastry, thawed
75 g (3 oz) sugar
170 ml (6 fl oz)
  double cream,
  whipped
50 g (2 oz)
  strawberries,
  halved
icing sugar for
  dredging

Roll out the pastry on a well sugared surface to a rectangle about 30 x 25 cm (12 x 10 inches).

Sprinkle with the sugar and press it in with a rolling pin. Take the shorter edge of the pastry and roll it up to the centre. Roll the other side to meet it at the centre. Moisten with water and press together to join the rolls. Cut into 1 cm (½ inch) slices and place well apart, cut side down on a dampened baking sheet, flattening them slightly.

Bake in a preheated hot oven, 220°C (425°F), Gas Mark 7, for 12 to 15 minutes; turn the palmiers over when they begin to brown, so that both sides caramelize. Transfer to a wire rack to cool. Spoon the cream into a piping bag fitted with a 1 cm (½ inch) fluted nozzle and pipe swirls of cream onto half of the palmiers. Arrange a few strawberries on the cream and top with the remaining palmiers. Press down and sprinkle with icing sugar.
Makes 6

Mille Feuilles

212 g (7½ oz) packet frozen puff pastry, thawed
125 g (4 oz) icing sugar, sifted
1 tablespoon water
3 tablespoons redcurrant jelly
3 tablespoons strawberry jam
170 ml (6 fl oz) double cream, whipped

Roll out the pastry into a large thin sheet, prick all over and cut into 15 pieces 10 x 6 cm (4 x 2½ inches). Place on dampened baking sheets and chill for 15 minutes.

Bake in a preheated hot oven, 220°C (425°F), Gas Mark 7, for 8 to 10 minutes until dark golden brown. Transfer to a wire rack to cool then split each piece in half.

Mix the icing sugar with the water to make a smooth icing and spread over the underside of 10 pastry slices. Place the redcurrant jelly in a piping bag fitted with a 5 mm (¼ inch) plain nozzle and pipe lines horizontally across the icing at 1 cm (½ inch) intervals. Take a skewer and draw it across from left to right and right to left in alternate lines to achieve a marbled effect. Set aside.

Cover another 10 pastry pieces with jam and cream. Place the remaining pastry pieces on top and cover with more jam and cream. Top with the iced pastry and press down firmly.

Makes 10

BREADS & TEABREADS

Soda Bread

1 kg (2 lb) plain flour
2 teaspoons salt
1 teaspoon bicarbonate of soda
1 teaspoon cream of tartar
50 g (2 oz) butter or margarine
600 ml (1 pint) buttermilk
flour for sprinkling

Sift the dry ingredients into a mixing bowl and rub in the fat. Add the buttermilk and mix quickly to a soft dough. Turn onto a floured surface, knead lightly and divide in half. Shape each half into a round about 5 cm (2 inches) thick and place on a floured baking sheet. Cut a deep cross on the top of each loaf and sprinkle with flour.

Bake in a preheated hot oven, 220°C (425°F), Gas Mark 7, for 25 to 30 minutes. Transfer to a wire rack to cool.

Makes two 500 g (1 lb) loaves

Malt Loaf

550 g (1 lb 2 oz) plain flour
1 teaspoon salt
50 g (2 oz) soft brown sugar
125 g (4 oz) currants
125 g (4 oz) sultanas
25 g (1 oz) chopped mixed peel
25 g (1 oz) fresh yeast
250 ml (8 fl oz) warm milk
50 g (2 oz) butter or margarine
4 tablespoons malt extract
2 tablespoons clear honey to glaze

Place all the dry ingredients in a bowl. Cream the yeast with a little of the milk and set aside. Add the fat and malt extract to the remaining milk and heat until melted. Cool slightly, then add to the dry ingredients with the yeast.

Beat to a soft dough, cover with a damp cloth and leave to rise in a warm place until doubled in size. Turn out and knead for 5 minutes until smooth. Divide in half and place in two 500 g (1 lb) greased loaf tins. Cover and leave in a warm place for about 1 hour until the dough reaches the top of the tins.

Bake in a preheated moderately hot oven, 190°C (375°F), Gas Mark 5, for 35 to 40 minutes until the bread sounds hollow when tapped. Turn onto a wire rack, then brush with honey.

Makes two 500 g (1 lb) loaves

Wholewheat Soda Bread

250 g (8 oz) plain
  flour
1 teaspoon
  bicarbonate of soda
2 teaspoons cream of
  tartar
2 teaspoons salt
350 g (12 oz)
  wholewheat flour
300 ml (½ pint)
  milk
4 tablespoons water
plain flour for
  sprinkling

Sift the dry ingredients into a mixing bowl. Mix in the wholewheat flour then add the milk and water and mix to a soft dough. Turn onto a floured surface, knead lightly, then shape into a large round about 5 cm (2 inches) thick. Place on a floured baking sheet, cut a deep cross on the top of the loaf and sprinkle with flour. Bake in a preheated hot oven, 220°C (425°F), Gas Mark 7, for 25 to 30 minutes. Transfer to a wire rack to cool.
Makes one 20 cm (8 inch) loaf

Granary Bread

500 g (1 lb) granary flour
1 teaspoon salt
15 g (½ oz) fresh yeast
300 ml (½ pint) warm water
1 tablespoon malt extract
1 tablespoon oil
cracked wheat

Mix the flour and salt in a bowl. Cream the yeast with a little of the water and leave until frothy. Add to the flour with the remaining water, malt extract and oil and mix to a dough.

Turn onto a floured surface and knead for 5 minutes until smooth and elastic. Place in a clean bowl, cover with a damp cloth and leave in a warm place to rise until doubled in size. Turn onto a floured surface and knead for 2 minutes. Shape into a round and place on a greased baking sheet. Brush with water and sprinkle with cracked wheat. Cover and leave in a warm place for about 30 minutes, until almost doubled in size.

Bake in a preheated hot oven, 220°C (425°F), Gas Mark 7, for 35 minutes, or until it sounds hollow when tapped. Cool on a wire rack.
Makes one loaf

Wholewheat Bread

1.5 kg (3 lb) wholewheat flour
1 tablespoon salt
25 g (1 oz) butter
25 g (1 oz) fresh yeast
900 ml – 1.2 litres (1½ – 2 pints) warm water
2 tablespoons malt extract
1 tablespoon cracked wheat

Mix the flour and salt together and rub in the butter. Mix the yeast with a little of the water and leave for 10 minutes. Mix the malt extract with the remaining water, add to the flour with the yeast and mix to a smooth dough.

Turn onto a floured surface and knead for 8 to 10 minutes until smooth and elastic. Place in a clean bowl, cover with a damp cloth and leave to rise in a warm place for about 2 hours until doubled in size.

Turn onto a floured surface, knead for a few minutes then divide into 4 pieces and place in greased 500 g (1 lb) loaf tins or clean greased clay flower pots. Brush with water and sprinkle with cracked wheat.

Cover and leave in a warm place for about 30 minutes until the dough just reaches the top of the tins. Bake in a preheated hot oven, 220°C (425°F), Gas Mark 7, for 30 to 40 minutes, or until the bread sounds hollow when tapped. Transfer to a wire rack to cool.

Makes four 500 g (1 lb) loaves

Basic White Bread

25 g (1 oz) fresh yeast
1 teaspoon caster sugar
900 ml (1 ½ pints) warm water
1.5 kg (3 lb) plain flour
1 tablespoon salt
1 tablespoon oil
flour for sprinkling

Cream the yeast with the sugar and a little of the water and leave for 10 minutes. Sift the flour and salt into a mixing bowl. Make a well in the centre and pour in the yeast, remaining water and oil. Mix to a smooth dough.

Turn onto a floured surface and knead for 8 to 10 minutes until smooth and elastic. Place in a clean bowl, cover with a damp cloth and leave to rise in a warm place for about 2 hours until doubled in size.

Turn onto a floured surface, knead for a few minutes, then divide in half and place in two greased 1 kg (2 lb) loaf tins. Make a cut along each loaf.
·Alternatively shape into rounds or cottage loaves and place on a floured baking sheet. Cover and leave in a warm place for 30 minutes until risen to the top of the tins.

Sprinkle with flour and bake in a preheated hot oven, 220°C (425°F), Gas Mark 7, for 35 to 40 minutes or until the bread sounds hollow when tapped. Cool on a wire rack.
Makes two 1 kg (2 lb) loaves

Milk Rolls

300 ml (½ pint) milk
50 g (2 oz) butter or margarine
15 g (½ oz) fresh yeast
1 teaspoon caster sugar
500 g (1 lb) plain flour
1 teaspoon salt
1 small egg, beaten
TO FINISH:
beaten egg
poppy seeds

Place the milk and fat in a pan and heat until lukewarm. Cream the yeast and sugar together, add a little of the warm milk and leave until frothy.

Sift the flour and salt into a warm bowl. Make a well in the centre and pour in the yeast, milk mixture and egg. Mix to a soft dough, then knead well until smooth and elastic.

Place in a clean bowl, cover with a damp cloth and leave to rise in a warm place for about 30 minutes until doubled in size. Turn onto a well-floured surface and knead for 2 to 3 minutes. Cut into 14 pieces and shape into rolls.

Place on a greased baking sheet, cover and leave in a warm place until doubled in size, about 10 to 15 minutes. Glaze with beaten egg, sprinkle with poppy seeds and bake in a preheated hot oven, 220°C (425°F), Gas Mark 7, for 20 minutes. Cool on a wire rack.
Makes 14

Hot Cross Buns

500 g (1 lb) plain flour
1 teaspoon salt
1 teaspoon ground mixed spice
2 teaspoons ground cinnamon
50 g (2 oz) soft brown sugar
50 g (2 oz) butter or margarine
25 g (1 oz) yeast
175 ml (6 fl oz) warm milk
1 large egg
75 g (3 oz) currants
25 g (1 oz) chopped mixed peel
PASTE:
3 tablespoons plain flour
2 tablespoons milk
1 teaspoon oil
GLAZE:
2 tablespoons milk
2 tablespoons caster sugar

Sift the flour, salt, spices and sugar into a mixing bowl and rub in the fat. Cream the yeast with a little of the milk and leave until frothy. Make a well in the centre of the dry ingredients, pour in the yeast, add the egg, fruit and remaining milk and mix together to make a smooth dough.

Turn onto a floured surface and knead for 8 minutes until smooth and elastic. Place in a clean bowl, cover with a damp cloth and leave to rise in a warm place for about 2 hours until doubled in size. Turn onto a floured surface and knead for 2 minutes. Divide into 12 pieces, shape into buns and place on a greased baking sheet. Cover and leave in a warm place for about 25 minutes until doubled in size.

To make the paste, put the flour in a small bowl and gradually stir in the milk and oil to make a smooth thick batter. Spoon into a small piping bag fitted with a 5 mm (¼ inch) plain nozzle and pipe a cross on the top of each bun. Bake in a preheated moderately hot oven, 200°C (400°F), Gas Mark 6, for 20 minutes until golden brown.

Place the milk and sugar in a small pan, bring to the boil and simmer for 2 minutes. Brush the buns with the glaze as soon as they come out of the oven. Transfer to a wire rack and cool slightly before serving.

Makes 12

Irish Brack

500 g (1 lb) mixed fruit
200 g (7 oz) soft brown sugar
300 ml (½ pint) cold tea
1 egg, beaten
275 g (9 oz) self-raising flour

Put the fruit, sugar and tea in a bowl and leave for 3 hours or until the tea is absorbed. Beat in the egg and flour.

Pour into a lined and greased 1 kg (2 lb) loaf tin and bake in a preheated moderate oven, 180°C (350°F), Gas Mark 4, for 1½ to 2 hours. Leave in the tin for 5 minutes, then cool on a wire rack. Serve sliced, with butter.
Makes one 1 kg (2 lb) loaf

Fig Loaf

250 g (8 oz) dried figs, chopped
125 g (4 oz) soft brown sugar
250 g (8 oz) All-Bran
2 tablespoons black treacle
600 ml (1 pint) cold tea
4 teaspoons baking powder
250 g (8 oz) wholewheat flour

Place the figs, sugar, All-Bran, treacle and tea in a mixing bowl and leave to stand for 1 hour. Sift in the baking powder, add the flour and mix together thoroughly.

Turn into a lined and greased 1 kg (2 lb) loaf tin and bake in a preheated moderate oven, 180°C (350°F), Gas Mark 4, for 1¼ to 1½ hours.

Turn onto a wire rack to cool. Serve sliced, with butter.
Makes one 1 kg (2 lb) loaf

Date Loaf

250 g (8 oz) dates, chopped
175 ml (6 fl oz) cold tea
250 g (8 oz) wholewheat flour
4 teaspoons baking powder
1 teaspoon ground mixed spice
175 g (6 oz) soft brown sugar
1 egg
TOPPING:
1 tablespoon demerara sugar

Put the dates in a bowl, pour over the tea and leave to soak for 2 hours. Add the remaining ingredients and mix thoroughly.

Turn into a lined and greased 1 kg (2 lb) loaf tin. Sprinkle with the demerara sugar and bake in a preheated moderate oven, 180°C (350°F), Gas Mark 4, for 1 to 1¼ hours.

Leave in the tin for 5 minutes, then turn onto a wire rack to cool. Serve sliced, spread with butter.
Makes one 1 kg (2 lb) loaf

Bran Bread

125 g (4 oz) All-Bran
75 g (3 oz) soft brown sugar
125 g (4 oz) mixed dried fruit
300 ml (½ pint) milk
125 g (4 oz) self-raising flour, sifted

Place the All-Bran, sugar, fruit and milk in a mixing bowl and leave to stand for 1 hour. Mix in the flour.

Turn into a lined and greased 500 g (1 lb) loaf tin and bake in a preheated moderate oven, 180°C (350°F), Gas Mark 4, for 55 to 60 minutes. Turn onto a wire rack to cool. Serve sliced, with butter.
Makes one 500 g (1 lb) loaf

Banana and Walnut Loaf

250 g (8 oz) self-raising flour
½ teaspoon ground cinnamon
125 g (4 oz) butter or margarine
125 g (4 oz) soft brown sugar
2 large eggs
3 large bananas, mashed
75 g (3 oz) walnuts, chopped

Grease and line a 1 kg (2 lb) loaf tin. Sift the flour with the cinnamon.

Cream the fat and sugar together until light and fluffy. Beat in the eggs one at a time, then the bananas. Fold in the flour and walnuts.

Pour into the prepared tin and bake in a preheated moderate oven, 180°C (350°F), Gas Mark 4, for 1 to 1¼ hours. Leave in the tin for 2 minutes then turn onto a wire rack to cool. Serve sliced, with butter.
Makes one 1 kg (2 lb) loaf

Ginger and Cherry Loaf

175 g (6 oz) plain flour
1½ teaspoons baking powder
2 teaspoons ground ginger
75 g (3 oz) butter
50 g (2 oz) crystallized ginger, chopped
75 g (3 oz) glacé cherries, chopped
75 g (3 oz) soft brown sugar
6 tablespoons milk

Sift the dry ingredients into a mixing bowl and rub in the fat until the mixture resembles breadcrumbs. Stir in the chopped ginger, cherries and sugar, then add the milk and mix to a stiff dough.

Turn into a greased and lined 500 g (1 lb) loaf tin and bake in a preheated moderate oven, 180°C (350°F), Gas Mark 4, for 1 to 1¼ hours. Turn onto a wire rack to cool. Serve sliced, with butter.
Makes one 500 g (1 lb) loaf

Fruit Plait

ENRICHED DOUGH:
250 g (8 oz) plain flour
½ teaspoon salt
15 g (½ oz) fresh yeast
6 tablespoons warm milk
50 g (2 oz) butter or margarine
1 egg, beaten
50 g (2 oz) caster sugar

FILLING:
500 g (1 lb) apples, peeled, cored and chopped
125 g (4 oz) sultanas
125 g (4 oz) soft brown sugar
1 teaspoon ground mixed spice

ICING:
75 g (3 oz) icing sugar
1 teaspoon water

Sift the flour and salt into a mixing bowl. Cream the yeast with a little of the milk. Melt the fat and add to the flour with the yeast, egg, sugar and remaining milk and mix to a smooth dough. Turn onto a floured surface and knead for 10 minutes until smooth and elastic. Place in a bowl, cover with a damp cloth and leave in a warm place for about 2 hours until doubled in size.

Meanwhile, prepare the filling. Place all the ingredients in a saucepan and cook until pulpy. Turn onto a plate and leave to cool.

Turn the dough onto a floured surface and knead for 2 minutes. Roll into an oblong 35 x 20 cm (14 x 8 inches) and spread the filling down the centre 7.5 cm (3 inches). Make slanting cuts 5 cm (2 inches) long at 2.5 cm (1 inch) intervals at each side of the filling. Take a strip from each side and cross them over the filling to make a plait. Tuck the last two strips underneath and seal with water.

Place on a greased baking sheet. Cover and leave in a warm place for about 30 minutes until doubled in size. Bake in a preheated moderately hot oven, 200°C (400°F), Gas Mark 6, for 30 to 35 minutes. Transfer to a wire rack to cool.

Mix the icing sugar with the water and brush over the plait while still warm.

Makes one 35 cm (14 inch) plait

Coconut Loaf

125 g (4 oz) butter or margarine
125 g (4 oz) caster sugar
2 eggs
175 g (6 oz) self-raising flour, sifted
4 tablespoons desiccated coconut
2 tablespoons milk

Cream the fat and sugar together until light and fluffy. Beat in the eggs one at a time, adding a little of the flour with the second. Fold in the remaining flour, 3 tablespoons of the coconut and the milk.

Turn into a lined and greased 500 g (1 lb) loaf tin and sprinkle with the remaining coconut. Bake in a preheated moderate oven, 180°C (350°F), Gas Mark 4, for 1 to 1¼ hours. Turn out and cool on a wire rack.

Makes one 500 g (1 lb) loaf

Swedish Tea Ring

ENRICHED DOUGH:
250 g (8 oz) plain flour
½ teaspoon salt
15 g (½ oz) fresh yeast
6 tablespoons warm milk
50 g (2 oz) butter
1 egg, beaten
50 g (2 oz) caster sugar

FILLING:
50 g (2 oz) butter, softened
75 g (3 oz) demerara sugar
50 g (2 oz) glacé cherries, chopped
50 g (2 oz) raisins
1 teaspoon ground cinnamon

DECORATION:
125 g (4 oz) icing sugar
1 tablespoon lemon juice
25 g (1 oz) walnuts
25 g (1 oz) glacé cherries
15 g (½ oz) angelica

Make the enriched dough as for Fruit Plait (page 78) and leave to rise until doubled in size.

Turn onto a floured surface and knead for 2 minutes, then roll out to 25 x 46 cm (10 x 18 inches).

Spread with the softened butter, then sprinkle with the sugar, fruit and cinnamon. Roll up tightly from the long side, dampen the edges and seal together well. Place on a greased baking sheet with the seam underneath and form into a ring, joining the ends together. Using scissors, make slanting cuts two-thirds through the ring at 2.5 cm (1 inch) intervals and turn each section on its side.

Cover and leave in a warm place for about 30 minutes until doubled in size, then bake in a preheated moderately hot oven, 200°C (400°F), Gas Mark 6, for 30 minutes. Transfer to a wire rack to cool.

Mix the icing sugar with the lemon juice and pour over the ring while still warm. Decorate with the walnuts, cherries and angelica.
Makes one tea ring

Chelsea Buns

ENRICHED DOUGH:
250 g (8 oz) plain flour
½ teaspoon salt
15 g (½ oz) fresh yeast
90 ml (3 fl oz) warm milk
50 g (2 oz) butter or margarine
1 egg, beaten
50 g (2 oz) caster sugar

FILLING:
50 g (2 oz) butter or margarine
50 g (2 oz) demerara sugar
125 g (4 oz) currants
1 teaspoon ground mixed spice

GLAZE:
3 tablespoons caster sugar
3 tablespoons water

Make the enriched dough as for Fruit Plait (page 78) and leave to rise until doubled in size. Turn onto a floured surface and knead for 2 minutes, then roll out to 30 x 23 cm (12 x 9 inches).

Melt the fat and brush over the dough, then sprinkle with the demerara sugar, fruit and spice. Roll up lengthwise like a Swiss roll, ending with the join underneath. Cut into 9 pieces and place cut side downwards in a greased 18 cm (7 inch) square cake tin.

Cover and leave in a warm place for 20 minutes until almost doubled in size. Bake in a preheated moderately hot oven, 200°C (400°F), Gas Mark 6, for 20 to 25 minutes until golden.

Meanwhile, dissolve the caster sugar in the water, then boil for 2 minutes. Brush the buns as soon as they come out of the oven. Transfer to a wire rack to cool.
Makes 9

FESTIVE & NOVELTY CAKES

Chocolate Log

SWISS ROLL:
3 large eggs
125 g (4 oz) caster sugar
50 g (2 oz) plain flour
25 g (1 oz) cocoa
1 tablespoon hot water

FUDGE ICING:
75 g (3 oz) butter
3 tablespoons milk
2 tablespoons cocoa
300 g (10 oz) icing sugar

TO FINISH:
icing sugar

Prepare and bake the Swiss roll as for Swiss Roll (page 13), sifting in the cocoa with the flour. Make the fudge icing as for Devil's Food Cake (page 18). Turn the sponge upside down onto sugared greaseproof paper, peel off the lining paper and trim the edges. Roll up with the sugared paper inside and allow to cool. Unroll and remove the paper, spread with some of the warm fudge icing and roll up like a Swiss roll. Leave the rest of the icing to cool.

Cut a short diagonal wedge off one end of the roll and join it to the side of the log with icing to resemble a branch. Place on a cake board. Cover the log with the cooled icing and mark lines with a fork to resemble the bark of a tree. Sprinkle with icing sugar to look like snow and decorate as liked, with a robin, holly, etc.

Makes one chocolate log

Snowman

175 g (6 oz) butter or margarine
175 g (6 oz) caster sugar
3 eggs
250 g (8 oz) self-raising flour
2 tablespoons hot water

ICING:
175 g (6 oz) caster sugar
1 egg white
2 tablespoons hot water
pinch of cream of tartar

Prepare the cake mixture as for Victoria Sandwich (page 8). Grease and flour a 300 ml (½ pint) and a 900 ml (1½ pint) pudding basin and fill each with the mixture. Bake in a preheated moderate oven, 160°C (325°F), Gas Mark 3, for 1 to 1¼ hours for the small cake, and 1½ to 1¾ hours for the large one. Turn onto a wire rack to cool.

Put the icing ingredients in a bowl over a pan of hot water and whisk for about 5 minutes until thick. Trim the small cake into a ball shape. Cover both cakes with icing. Place the large cake upside down on a cake board and place the small one on top for the head.

Decorate as desired with hat, scarf, pipe, sweets, etc.
Makes one snowman

Christmas Cake

275 g (9 oz) plain flour
1 teaspoon ground mixed spice
½ teaspoon grated nutmeg
250 g (8 oz) butter or margarine
250 g (8 oz) soft brown sugar
grated rind of 1 lemon
1 tablespoon treacle
5 large eggs
75 g (3 oz) ground almonds
350 g (12 oz) currants
250 g (8 oz) sultanas
175 g (6 oz) raisins
125 g (4 oz) glacé cherries, quartered
75 g (3 oz) chopped mixed peel
50 g (2 oz) split almonds, chopped

ALMOND PASTE:
500 g (1 lb) ground almonds
250 g (8 oz) icing sugar
250 g (8 oz) caster sugar
1 large egg
2 teaspoons lemon juice
4 drops of almond essence
4 tablespoons warmed, sieved apricot jam

ROYAL ICING:
3 egg whites
750 g (1½ lb) icing sugar, sifted
1 teaspoon lemon juice
2 teaspoons glycerine

Prepare a deep 23 cm (9 inch) cake tin as for Boiled Fruit Cake (page 17).

Make the cake as for Dundee Cake (page 16), adding the treacle with the fat and sugar, and the ground and chopped almonds with the fruit.

Turn into the prepared tin and smooth the top. Bake in a preheated cool oven, 150°C (300°F), Gas Mark 2, for 3 to 4 hours; test with a skewer after 3 hours. Leave in the tin for 10 minutes, then turn onto a wire rack to cool.

(If liked, when cold, make a few holes in the top of the cake with a skewer and pour over 2 tablespoons brandy.) Wrap in double greaseproof paper and store in an airtight tin for at least 2 weeks before using.

TO ALMOND PASTE THE CAKE
Mix the almonds and sugars together, add the egg, lemon juice and essence and mix to a smooth pliable paste. Brush the cake with apricot jam.

Roll out just over half the almond paste into a 23 cm (9 inch) circle and place on top of the cake. Roll out the remaining paste into 2 strips the depth and half the circumference of the cake. Place these round the side of the cake and press together. Stand on a cake board and leave in a dry place for 2 to 3 days before icing.

TO ICE THE CAKE
Lightly whisk the egg whites, then add the icing sugar a little at a time, beating well between each addition, until the icing is smooth and stiff enough to form peaks. Beat in the lemon juice and glycerine.

Spread the icing over the cake and draw up into peaks to look like snow. Decorate with holly, robin, etc. as desired.

Makes one 25 cm (10 inch) cake

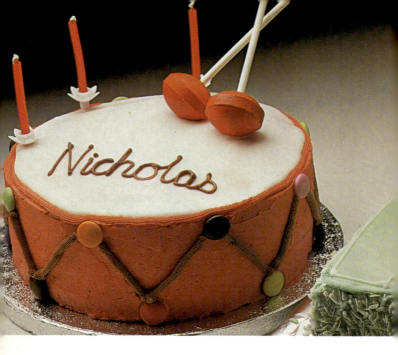

Drum Cake

125 g (4 oz) butter or margarine
125 g (4 oz) caster sugar
2 eggs
125 g (4 oz) self-raising flour, sifted
1 tablespoon hot water
BUTTER ICING:
75 g (3 oz) butter
250 g (8 oz) icing sugar, sifted
2 tablespoons milk
red food colouring
GLACÉ ICING:
250 g (8 oz) icing sugar, sifted
2 tablespoons water
TO DECORATE:
1 teaspoon cocoa
smarties
2 lollipops

Prepare and bake the cake as for Victoria Sandwich (page 8). Make the butter icing as for Coffee Walnut Layer Cake (page 50), adding the colouring instead of the essence. Sandwich the cakes together with icing, stand on a cake board and cover the sides with the remaining butter icing.

To make the glacé icing, mix the icing sugar and water until smooth. Spread three-quarters over the top of the cake and leave to set.

Add the cocoa to the remaining glacé icing and put into a piping bag fitted with a plain writing nozzle. Place 8 smarties around the side of the cake at the top and another 8 at the bottom, midway between those at the top.

Pipe diagonal lines of chocolate icing to join the smarties top to bottom. Place the lollipops on top for drumsticks.
Makes one drum cake

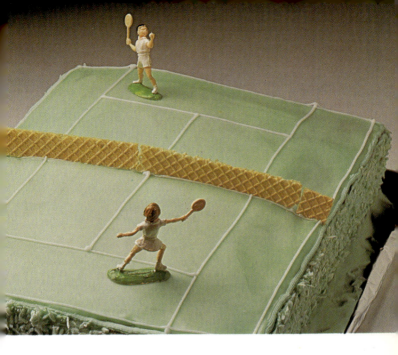

Tennis Cake

250 g (8 oz) butter or margarine
250 g (8 oz) caster sugar
4 eggs
250 g (8 oz) self-raising flour
2 tablespoons hot water
BUTTER ICING:
75 g (3 oz) butter
250 g (8 oz) icing sugar, sifted
2 tablespoons milk
green food colouring
GLACÉ ICING:
250 g (8 oz) icing sugar, sifted
2 tablespoons water
TO DECORATE:
50 g (2 oz) desiccated coconut
wafers

Line and grease two 18 x 28 cm (7 x 11 inch) Swiss roll tins. Prepare and bake the cakes as for Victoria Sandwich (page 8).

Make the butter icing as for Coffee Walnut Layer Cake (page 50), adding the colouring instead of the essence. Sandwich the cakes together with icing and place on a cake board. Spread the remaining icing over the sides of the cake. Colour the coconut green and press onto the sides.

Make the glacé icing, keep a little aside, colour the rest green and use to coat the top. Leave to set.

Fit a small piping bag with a plain writing nozzle and fill with the white glacé icing. Pipe white lines on the cake as for a tennis court. Cut the wafers into 2.5 cm (1 inch) strips and place across the centre for a net. Put toy figures on court if liked.
Makes one tennis cake

Hedgehog

1 tablespoon cocoa
2 tablespoons hot water
125 g (4 oz) margarine
125 g (4 oz) caster sugar
2 eggs
125 g (4 oz) self-raising flour
BUTTER ICING:
2 tablespoons cocoa
3 tablespoons hot water
75 g (3 oz) butter
250 g (8 oz) icing sugar
TO DECORATE:
50 g (2 oz) shredded almonds
3 smarties

Prepare and bake the cake as for Castle Cake (page 89), using a 20 cm (8 inch) sandwich tin. Make the icing as for Devil's Food Cake (page 18).

Cut the cake vertically in half to make two semi-circles and sandwich together with some of the icing. To form the nose, cut 2 diagonal slices from each side of the front of the cake and discard. Stand the flat edge on a cake board and cover the cake with icing.

Smooth the icing over the nose and face and fork lines from front to back over the rest of the 'hedgehog'. Stick in the almond strips at random to represent prickles. Use the smarties for the nose and eyes.

Makes one 'hedgehog'

Castle Cake

25 g (1 oz) cocoa
3 tablespoons hot water
175 g (6 oz) margarine
175 g (6 oz) caster sugar
3 eggs
175 g (6 oz) self-raising flour, sifted
BUTTER ICING:
2 tablespoons cocoa
3 tablespoons hot water
75 g (3 oz) butter
250 g (8 oz) icing sugar
TO DECORATE:
wafers
wafer-thin chocolate mints

Line and grease an 18 x 28 cm (7 x 11 inch) Swiss roll tin, leaving 2.5 cm (1 inch) paper above the sides.

Blend the cocoa with the water; cool slightly. Cream the fat and sugar until light and fluffy; beat in the cocoa.

Beat in the eggs one at a time, adding a tablespoon of the flour with the last two. Fold in the remaining flour and turn into the prepared tin. Bake in a preheated moderately hot oven, 190°C (375°F), Gas Mark 5, for 25 to 30 minutes. Turn onto a wire rack to cool.

Make the icing as for Devil's Food Cake (page 18).

Cut a 3.5 cm (1½ inch) strip from one end of the cake and cut into 4 squares. Cut the remaining cake in half and sandwich together with icing. Cover the top and sides of the cake with icing, smooth, then mark lines for bricks. Cover the squares with the remaining icing and place on the corners for turrets.

Cut the wafers to make windows and a door and place in position. Cut the mints into small squares and place between the turrets for battlements. Finish with flags at each corner and toy soldiers.

Makes one castle cake

21st Birthday Cake

325 g (11 oz) plain flour
2 teaspoons ground mixed spice
½ teaspoon grated nutmeg
300 g (10 oz) butter or margarine
300 g (10 oz) soft brown sugar
grated rind of 1 lemon
2 tablespoons black treacle
6 eggs
75 g (3 oz) ground almonds
500 g (1 lb) currants
325 g (11 oz) sultanas
175 g (6 oz) raisins
125 g (4 oz) glacé cherries, quartered
125 g (4 oz) chopped mixed peel
125 g (4 oz) split almonds, chopped

ALMOND PASTE:
525 g (1¼ lb) ground almonds
300 g (10 oz) caster sugar
300 g (10 oz) icing sugar
2 eggs
2 teaspoons lemon juice
½ teaspoon almond essence
4 tablespoons warmed, sieved apricot jam

Prepare a deep 23 cm (9 inch) square cake tin as for Boiled Fruit Cake (page 17). Make, bake and store the cake as for Dundee Cake (page 16), adding the treacle with the fat and sugar and the chopped and ground almonds with the fruit.

Make the almond paste and cover the cake as for Christmas Cake (page 84).

Make the royal icing as for Christmas Cake. Put half the icing on top of the cake, keeping the rest covered with a damp cloth. Spread the icing over the top of the cake with a palette knife. Pull an icing ruler over the icing to make a smooth flat surface. Remove any excess icing and leave for 24 hours.

Spread two-thirds of the remaining icing around the sides of the cake, and smooth with a palette knife. Remove surplus icing from the bottom and top edges and leave to set for 24 hours.

Place the remaining icing in a piping bag fitted with a plain writing nozzle and decorate the cake with a lattice pattern (as shown). Pipe lines at 5 mm (¼ inch) intervals diagonally across the corners, then pipe lines across these at right angles. When dry, pipe lines at right angles on top of these, but slightly longer to make a neat finish.

To form the lattice at the bottom of the cake, pipe lines from the board about 1 cm (½ inch) away from the cake diagonally 1 cm (½ inch) up the cake. Repeat the lines at 1 cm (½ inch) intervals all round the cake, then pipe a second set of lines diagonally opposite. When dry pipe another line on top. Using a small shell pipe, pipe a border of shells along the edge of the lattice.

ROYAL ICING:
5 egg whites
1.25 kg (2½ lb) icing sugar
2 teaspoons lemon juice
3 teaspoons glycerine
few drops of food colouring

Colour a little of the icing, put into a small icing bag fitted with a writing nozzle and pipe 21 on top of the cake. Decorate the sides with sugar roses, if liked.

Makes one 25 cm (10 inch) cake

Simnel Cake

200 g (7 oz) plain flour
2 teaspoons ground mixed spice
175 g (6 oz) butter or margarine
175 g (6 oz) soft brown sugar
grated rind of 1 orange
4 eggs
175 g (6 oz) currants
175 g (6 oz) sultanas
175 g (6 oz) raisins
75 g (3 oz) glacé cherries, quartered
50 g (2 oz) chopped mixed peel

ALMOND PASTE:
350 g (12 oz) ground almonds
175 g (6 oz) icing sugar
175 g (6 oz) caster sugar
1 large egg
4 drops of almond essence
2 teaspoons lemon juice
1 tablespoon warmed, sieved apricot jam

Prepare a 19 cm (7½ inch) cake tin as for Boiled Fruit Cake (page 17). Make the cake as for Dundee Cake (page 16). Make the almond paste as for Christmas Cake (page 84) and roll out one quarter into a 19 cm (7½ inch) circle.

Place half the cake mixture in the prepared tin, lay the circle of almond paste on top and press down lightly. Place the remaining cake mixture on top and smooth the surface.

Bake in a preheated moderate oven, 160°C (325°F), Gas Mark 3, for 1 hour, then lower the temperature to 150°C (300°F), Gas Mark 2 and bake for a further 2½ hours or until a skewer inserted into the centre comes out clean. Leave in the tin for 5 minutes then turn onto a wire rack to cool.

Roll one third of the remaining almond paste into a circle to fit the top of the cake. Brush the cake with apricot jam and press the paste into place. Shape the remaining paste into small balls and arrange around the top of the cake. Place under a hot grill to brown the balls. Tie a yellow ribbon round the cake and decorate as liked, with sweet eggs, etc.
Makes one 19 cm (7½ inch) cake

Easter Truffles

175 g (6 oz) plain chocolate
1 egg yolk
25 g (1 oz) butter
1 teaspoon coffee essence
1 tablespoon cocoa

Melt the chocolate in a bowl over a pan of hot water. Add the egg yolk, butter and coffee essence and leave in a cool place for 30 to 40 minutes until set.

Mould into small egg shapes with the fingers and roll in the cocoa to coat evenly.
Makes 20

INDEX

Almond curls 62
Almond galettes 25
Angel cake 9
Apple and cinnamon cake 10

Banana and walnut loaf 77
Banana cake 11
Birthday cake, 21st 90-91
Biscuits:
  Almond galettes 25
  Brownies 33
  Chocolate biscuit cake 34
  Chocolate caramel fingers 34
  Chocolate chip biscuits 28
  Chocolate crisps 37
  Chocolate crunch 33
  Cinnamon crisps 28
  Coconut cookies 28
  Coconut pyramids 33
  Date and oat slices 30
  Digestive biscuits 31
  Flapjacks 27
  Ginger nuts 36
  Macaroons 24
  Oat crunchies 26
  Shortbread 41
  Uncooked chocolate bars 37
  Walnut cookies 32
  Wholewheat biscuits 37
Boiled fruit cake 17
Brandy snaps 60
Breads:
  Basic white bread 71
  Bran bread 77
  Granary bread 69
  Malt loaf 67
  Milk rolls 72
  Soda bread 66
  Wholewheat bread 70
  Wholewheat soda bread 68
Brownies 33

Cakes & sponges, Family:
  Angel cake 9
  Apple and cinnamon cake 10
  Banana cake 11
  Cherry cake 14
  Chocolate almond cake 19
  Chocolate bars, Uncooked 37
  Chocolate cake 6
  Devil's food cake 18
  Dundee cake 16
  Fruit cakes 16,17,20,21
  Genoese sponge 12
  Ginger cake 7
  Madeira cake 15
  Marmalade cake 15
  Parkin 23
  Sticky gingerbread 22
  Swiss roll 13
  Victoria sandwich cake 8
  Whisked sponge 12
Caramel chip gâteau 48
Castle cake 89
Chelsea buns 81
Cherry cake 14
Chocolate almond cake 19
Chocolate and chestnut gâteau 42
Chocolate biscuit cake 34
Chocolate cake 6
Chocolate caramel fingers 34
Chocolate chip biscuits 28
Chocolate crisps 37
Chocolate crunch 33
Chocolate éclairs 57
Chocolate log 82
Christmas cake 84
Cinnamon crisps 28
Coconut cookies 28
Coconut loaf 79
Coconut pyramids 33
Coffee and walnut layer cake 50
Cream horns 58
Crystallized fruit cake 21

Date and oat slices 30
Date loaf 74
Devil's food cake 18
Digestive biscuits 31
Drum cake 86
Dundee cake 16

Easter truffles 92
Éclairs, Chocolate 57
Everyday fruit cake 20

Farmhouse fruit cake 16
Festive & novelty cakes 82-93
Fig loaf 74
Flapjacks 27

Florentines 53
Frangipane tartlets 61
Fruit plait 78

Gâteaux 42-51
  Apricot gâteau 51
  Caramel chip gâteau 48
  Chocolate and chestnut gâteau 42
  Coffee and walnut layer cake 50
  Gâteau au chocolat 44
  Gâteau aux fraises 46
  Gâteau aux noisettes 49
  Gâteau moka 47
  Gâteau normande 43
  Gâteau pithiviers 45
Genoese sponge 12
Ginger and cherry loaf 77
Ginger cake 7
Ginger nuts 36
Gingerbread, Sticky 22

Hedgehog 88
Hot cross buns 73

Irish brack 74

Japonais 56

Langues de chats 54

Macaroons 24
Madeira cake 15
Malt loaf 67
Marmalade cake 15
Meringues, Walnut 52
Mille feuilles 65
Mocha slices 54

Oat crunchies 26

Parkin 23
Pâtisserie & small cakes:
  Almond curls 62
  Brandy snaps 60
  Chocolate éclairs 57
  Cream horns 58
  Florentines 53
  Frangipane tartlets 61
  Japonais 56
  Langues de chats 54
  Mille feuilles 65
  Mocha slices 54
  Sponge fingers 62
  Strawberry palmiers 64
  Tartelettes aux fraises 58
  Tea-time truffles 62
  Viennese fingers 55
  Walnut barquettes 59
  Walnut meringues 52

Sandwich cake, Victoria 8
Scones 40:
  Cheese topped scones 39
  Drop scones 40
  Fruit scone round 38
Shortbread 41
Simnel cake 92
Small cakes *see* Pâtisserie
Snowman 83
Sponge fingers 62
Sponges *see* Cakes
Sticky gingerbread 22
Strawberry palmiers 64
Swedish tea ring 80
Swiss roll 13

Tartelettes aux fraises 58
Teabreads 66-81
Tennis cake 87
Truffles:
  Easter 92
  Tea-time 62
21st birthday cake 90-91

Victoria sandwich cake 8
Viennese fingers 55

Walnut barquettes 59
Walnut cookies 32
Walnut meringues 52
Whisked sponge 12
Wholewheat biscuits 37

Acknowledgments
Photography by Paul Williams
Food prepared by Carole Handslip
Designed by Astrid Publishing Consultants Ltd